This
ORCHARD CHILDREN'S TREASURY

belongs to

THE ORCHARD
CHILDREN'S TREASURY

THE OR

CHILDREN'S

CHARD

TREASURY

 ORCHARD BOOKS

Editor: Mandy Suhr
Art Director: Jemima Lumley

Editorial Assistant: Shaheen Bilgrami
Designers: Anna-Louise Billson, Lisa Nutt

First Published in 1997 by
ORCHARD BOOKS
96 Leonard Street, London EC2A 4RH
Orchard Books Australia
14 Mars Road, Lane Cove, NSW 2066
ISBN 1 86039 556 2
A CIP catalogue record for this book is available
from the British Library
Printed in Italy

With special thanks to all the authors
and illustrators who have contributed
to the Orchard list.

All those who tend the Orchard know
Each tree must discover its own way to grow –
And on each branch the books ripen and glow.

Adrian Mitchell

"Within the covers of a loved book is an adventure of the spirit..."

Liz Waterland

What better introduction to the magical world of books than sharing a story with a child, travelling together to a world of fantasy and fairy tale where dragons can be slain, villains outwitted, and adventures had, all from the safe confines of an armchair.

It is this kind of early apprenticeship which fosters a real and enduring love of books and reading, and which will equip a child with the confidence and skills to go on to read alone. Stories open up a whole new world, where children can explore their own feelings and those of others, as well as facing new or worrying situations – learning life skills which they will take on into young adulthood.

It was with this in mind that the ORCHARD CHILDREN'S TREASURY was created: a carefully chosen collection to take a child from the earliest months, and to grow with. Inside you will find baby books, picture books, rhymes, poems, fairytales, legends and classic stories, all featuring a colourful and appealing array of illustrations. There is something here for everyone: bold and exuberant work by exciting new artists, cleverly-crafted stories from best-selling contemporary authors, as well as stories and illustration from classic literature.

The ORCHARD CHILDREN'S TREASURY is divided into three sections to make it easy to dip into.

The first section, *The Nursery Years*, was collated with children of six months to three years in mind. It combines all the essential first learning and childhood experiences: first words, traditional rhymes, early learning concepts, counting and ABC, first experiences, and classic nursery and bedtime tales.

The second section, *The Early Years*, moves on from this solid foundation with a delightful collection of stories and poems, hand-picked not only for their humour, colourful illustrations, or clever storyline, but often because they explore the experiences or emotions of the young child.

The final section, *Stories For All*, contains stories and poems of appeal to children from six to a hundred! Here you will find myths, legends, and classic and traditional stories from all corners of the world, all eloquently retold and illustrated by some of today's most talented artists.

The ORCHARD CHILDREN'S TREASURY is a collection that we hope will delight readers of all ages, and one which will indeed be treasured and revisited throughout childhood.

THE NURS

CONT

ERY YEARS

ENTS

THE EARⁱ

CONTᵢ

~~EARL~~Y YEARS

~~CONT~~ENTS

STORIES
CONT

FOR ALL

‎ENTS

What are little boys made of?
What are little boys made of?
Bearhugs, banged shins
And ragamuffin grins,
That's what little boys are made of.

What are little girls made of?
What are little girls made of?
Grazed knees and wriggles,
And freckledy giggles,
That's what little girls are made of.

Lucy Coats

THE NURS

It is never too soon to introduce children to books. From the earliest months children respond with pleasure to the rhythmic and musical patterns of nursery rhymes. They soon begin to point out colours and shapes, and enjoy identifying images on a page, practising their own first words.

ERY YEARS

Later on, they will recognise familiar situations and emotions in a story, and use these to interpret their own world.

A warm and cosy story at bedtime is a wonderful way to introduce a young child to longer stories, and to nurture a vital love of books and reading.

Humpty Dumpty
and Other Rhymes

from The Orchard Book of Nursery Rhymes

Faith Jaques

Humpty Dumpty sat on a wall,
Humpty Dumpty had a great fall.
All the King's horses and all the King's men
Couldn't put Humpty together again.

Ring-a-ring o' roses,
A pocket full of posies,
A-tishoo! A-tishoo!
We all fall down.

Hey! diddle, diddle,

The cat and the fiddle,

The cow jumped over the moon.

The little dog laughed to see such sport,

And the dish ran away with the spoon.

This little pig went to market,

This little pig stayed at home,

This little pig had roast beef,

This little pig had none,

And this little pig cried,

Wee-wee-wee-wee-wee!

I can't find my way home.

Baa, baa, black sheep,
Have you any wool?
Yes, sir, yes, sir,
Three bags full.
One for the master,
And one for the dame,
And one for the little boy
Who lives down the lane.

There was an old woman who lived in a shoe,
She had so many children she didn't know what to do,
She gave them some broth without any bread;
She whipped them all soundly and put them to bed.

MY CLOTHES

• Venice Shone •

• shirt •

• t-shirt •

• hat •

• sandals •

• dungarees •

• socks •

• skirt •

• pants •

• slippers •

• shorts •

• jacket •

• jumper •

• raincoat •

• boots •

• mittens •

27

Getting Dressed

I can tie
my shoelaces

I can brush
my hair

I can wash my
hands and face

And dry myself
with care.

* Carol Thompson *

I can clean my
teeth, too

And fasten up
my frocks

I can dress all
by myself

And pull up both
my socks.

This Little Baby's
Potty

Lynn Breeze

This little baby's
getting dressed.

Mummy helps
with pants
and vest.

Running, jumping, feeling happy.

Nice and dry without a nappy!

Here's a boat
to sail the sea...

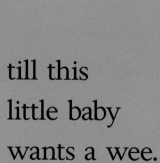

till this
little baby
wants a wee.

Run inside
as quick as
may be.

Use the potty,
clever baby!

One Hungry Baby

A Bedtime Counting Rhyme

Lucy Coats  Sue Hellard

One
hungry
baby ...

Two front teeth.

Three dribbly chins
with bibs underneath.

Four bubbly bathtimes
To wash off the crumbs.

Five sploshy splashers
Five wet mums.

Six funny dads
Drying six button noses.

Seven big sisters
Counting tails and toeses.

Eight fat teddies
Ready for bed.

Nine soft pillows
Nine sleepy heads.

Ten good babies
Tucked up tight.

Twenty tired parents
Waving goodnight.

Purple Sock, Pink Sock

Colours

Jonathan Allen

Little Tabby's getting
dressed. Pink sock…

Purple sock
what comes next?

Big red trousers
with red braces

New brown shoes
with long brown laces

Favourite T-shirt
clean and white

Old blue jumper
much too tight

Yellow coat with
yellow buttons

Then a pair of bright
green mittens

Orange scarf and
a big black hat

What a
colourful
Tabby Cat!

Five Little
DUCKS

IAN BECK

Five little ducks went swimming one day,
Over the hills and far away.

Mother duck said, "Quack, quack, quack, quack."
But only four little ducks came back.

Four little ducks went swimming one day,
Over the hills and far away.

Mother duck said, "Quack, quack, quack, quack." But only three little ducks came back.

Three little ducks went swimming one day,
Over the hills and far away.

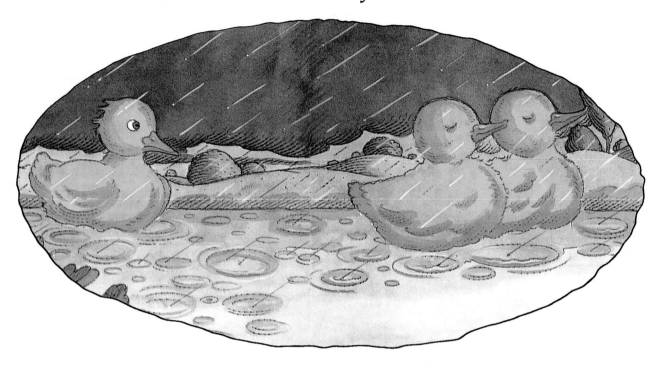

Mother duck said,
"Quack, quack,
quack, quack."
But only two little
ducks came back.

Two little ducks went swimming one day,
Over the hills and far away.

Mother duck said,
"Quack, quack,
quack, quack."
But only one little
duck came back.

One little duck went
swimming one day,

Over the hills

and far away.

Mother duck said, "Quack, quack, quack, quack."

And all her five
little ducks
came back.

Goes Shopping

Lynn Breeze

This little baby
skips and hops

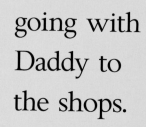

going with
Daddy to
the shops.

54

Here's a trolley
and the
shopping list;

apples, pears,
bananas: nothing
must be missed!

Big yellow cheeses
and biscuits
to crunch

honey for
breakfast and
beans for lunch.

Peep, peep,
goes the till.
Help to pack.

Carry the
shopping all
the way back.

Heads and Shoulders

Heads and shoulders
knees and toes.

* Carol Thompson *

And eyes and ears
and mouth and nose.

One·Two·Three How Many Animals Can You See?

Emilie Boon

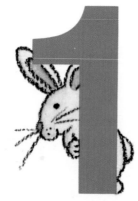

One! Two! Three!
How many animals can you see?
Run, Rabbit, run!
That's just one!

Fox trots behind.
That makes two.

Duck paddles up.
That makes three.

Otter pops out.
That makes four.

Mouse joins in.
That makes five.

6

Owl flies above.

That makes six.

Hedgehog bobs along.
That makes seven.

Deer's waiting here.
That makes eight.

Squirrel scrambles on.
That makes nine.

One! Two! Three!
How many animals can you see?
Bear counts them all again.
Eight! Nine! Ten!

· Helping ·

· Catherine Anholt ·

· tidying ·

· sweeping ·

· mixing ·

fetching ·

• holding •

• cleaning •

• planting •

• choosing •

I like helping!

Four Fierce Kittens

Joyce Dunbar Jakki Wood

Fat mother cat was asleep on her mat.

Said her four little kittens,

"There's no fun in that!"

And they went off round the farm to run wild.

Said the marmalade kitten,
spiking her claws,
"I am a terrible tiger!
I shall hunt hen out of her hutch."

And she tried to growl
(but she didn't know how)
She could only go...

miaow

miaow

And hen
went

CLUCK

CLUCK

CLUCK

Said the black little kitten,
with a glint in his eye,
"I am a panther on the prowl.
I shall frighten the pig out of his sty."

And he tried to howl
(But he didn't know how)
He could only go...

miaow
miaow

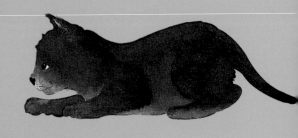

And pig
went

OINK

OINK

OINK

Said the tortoiseshell kitten,
pricking her ears,
"I am a leaping leopard!
I shall chase duck into her pond."

And she tried to snarl
(But she didn't know how)
She could only go...

miaow
miaow

And duck
went

QUACK

QUACK

QUACK

Said the tabby little kitten, twitching her tail,
"I am a dangerous lion!
I shall make the sheep run down the lane."

And she tried to roar
(But she didn't know how)
She could only go ...

miaow

miaow

And the
sheep went

BAA

BAA

BAA

Said the four little kittens, ever so fierce,
"We are tigers! Panthers! Leopards! Lions!
We shall scare that gaggle of geese!"

And they tried to roar,
To snarl, to growl
And they managed to go...

miaow

miaow

But the
geese went

HONK

HONK

HONK

Then a puppy came over to play.
Those four fierce kittens arched their backs.
Their fur stood on end. They hissed. They spat!
And that terrified puppy ran away ...

SCAT!

Said those
proud little
kittens,
"We didn't know
we could do
THAT!"

And they went back to their mother,
to sleep on the mat.

The Weather and Me

Jonathan Allen

by Fred Cat

FRED CAT'S
WEATHER

THE ·ORCHARD· ABC

·IAN·BECK·

A is for alligator, Aladdin, acrobat, apple, anchor, avocado and ant

B is for bear, Bo-peep, basket, baby, bird, balloon, butterfly, bricks, boat and ball

C is for cat, clown, crabs, cake, candle, cliffs and clouds

D is for duck, drum and daisies

Ee

E is for elephant, envelope and eggshell

F is for fox, flute, fountain, fireworks, frog and fan

G is for gorilla, guitar, goose, grapes, glasses and grass

H is for Humpty-Dumpty, hippopotamus, house, hen and hyacinths

Ii

I is for imp and ink

Jj

J is for Jack and Jill, Jack and the Beanstalk and Jack-in-the-box

Kk

K is for king, kangaroo, kiwi, koala, kite and key

L is for lion, Little Red Riding Hood, lemons, lighthouse, ladder, leaves and ladybird

Mm

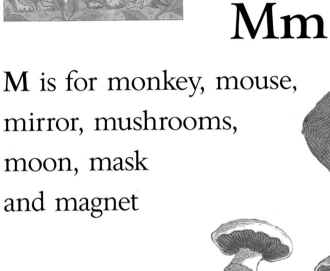

M is for monkey, mouse, mirror, mushrooms, moon, mask and magnet

N is for Noah's Ark

O is for Old King Cole,
ostrich, octopus, orange,
onion and owl

P is for Puss-in-Boots,
pig, pumpkin, parasol,
parrot, pears, pansies
and palace

Q is for queen,
quail, quill and
question mark

R is for robot, rocket, rocking-horse, rainbow, reins and rope

S is for sun, sea, sand, starfish, sandcastle, sailor, spade and star

T is for toad, toucan, teddy-bear, trumpet, Tom Thumb, tree and toothbrush

U is for unicorn,
umbrella and
Ugly Duckling

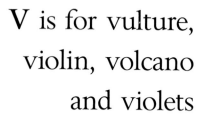

V is for vulture,
violin, volcano
and violets

W is for woodcutter,
woods, windmill,
witch and well

X is the ending for
fox and for box

Y is for yak, yawn,
yoghurt and yo-yo

Zz

Z is for zebras zzzz-ing

Going to Playgroup

Pictures by Catherine Anholt
Story by Laurence Anholt

Anna wasn't big enough to go to school. And she wasn't nearly big enough to go to work. But Mummy said she was getting too big to stay at home all day.

"It's time to make friends of your own," she said. "It's time to start at playgroup!"

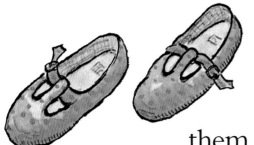

"You'll need new shoes for playgroup," said Mummy.

"Who will help me put them on?" said Anna.

"There will be a playleader, called Mrs Sams, and lots of other children," said Mummy.

"Supposing nobody likes me?" said Anna. She thought she'd take her sister with her. But babies don't go to playgroup.

"Perhaps I'll just stay at home," she said.

"Don't worry," said Mummy. "You'll love it when you get there."

"Hello," said Mrs Sams when they arrived.
"What lovely shoes. Shall I help you put them on?

This is where we hang our coats and this is
Tom. It's his first day too."

Mrs Sams took Anna and Tom to meet
the other children. Some were having a story,
and some were...

sticking

cutting

drawing

building

painting

and rolling.

Everyone was busy.

"Will you make something nice for me?" Mummy asked Anna. Then she went out of the door!

"Look, these teddies keep crying," said Tom. "They're being very naughty."

"Perhaps they miss their mummies," said Anna. "Shall we take them for a walk?"

Anna and Tom took their teddies to see...

the rabbits

the guinea pig

the sand box

the water

the bikes

the slide

the home
corner

the bookshelf

the dressing-up
clothes.

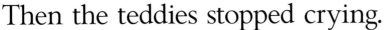

Then the teddies stopped crying.

Mrs Sams needed two helpers. All the children wanted to help. But Mrs Sams chose Anna and Tom. "You're both very helpful," she said.

Then all the children queued for the toilets ... but some people couldn't wait.

They all had to wash their hands. Tom forgot to pull up his sleeves.

"Now walk back quietly," said Mrs Sams. But some children ran.

"And try and sit still," said Mrs Sams. But everyone jumped about. Anna sat next to Tom.

The children sang some songs, and clapped their hands, and then they all ran outside to play until it was time to go home.

"Hello," said Mummy.
"Did you make
something nice?"
"Yes," said Anna.
"I made a friend!"

"Will it be playgroup again tomorrow?"

Big Owl, Little Towel

Big cat, little hat

Little cat, big hat

Big bear, little chair

Big chair, little bear

Sizes   by Jonathan Allen

Big owl, little towel

Big towel, little owl

Big mole, little hole

Big hole, little mole

Mr Bear's Plane

Colin & Jacqui Hawkins

Mr Bear pushed his red plane out of the garden shed.

It was brand new and he couldn't wait to try it.

"I think I might go for a flight," he said.

Mr Bear's friends arrived.

"Hello, again!"
"Is that a plane?"
"Gee whizz!"
"Yes, it is!"
"Doesn't it shine!"

"Yes," said Mr Bear, "and it's mine!"

"Why don't you get in? We can go for a spin!"

But his friends were all too busy.

"I'm fishing today. I really can't stay."

"It's time we went
to put up our tent."
"Let's get off quick!
Planes make me sick!"
"Up in the sky?
No! Pigs don't fly!"

"Bye, bye! I must
get my washing dry!"

**So Mr Bear decided
he would go on his
own.**

"Let's have a look.
It's all in this book.
One, two.
Here's what you do.
Three, four.
Engine's roar.
Five, six.
Pull on joystick.
Seven, eight.
I can hardly wait!
Nine, ten.
Let's go then!"

**With a mighty
roar the little
red plane leapt
into the air!**

"Wey hey! Wey ho!
Off we go!"

Round and round
the sky he flew
and then, far below,
he saw Croc, fishing.

"That's Croc
over there.
I'll give him
a scare!
Yoo, hoo!"

Mr Bear turned the
plane towards Croc.
It zoomed under the
bridge and caught
Croc's fishing line.
Croc reeled himself
aboard.

"Did you decide
to come for a ride?"
said Mr Bear.

"You gave me a fright!"
"You do look a sight!"
"Look, there's the rest
of the bunch."
"Let's drop in for lunch!"

Rhino, Elly and Piggy
were sitting by their
tent. They looked up
in horror as Mr Bear
and Croc swooped
down on them.

SCRUNCH! The tent
was ripped from
the ground.

"Look out, Mr Bear!"

"All aboard?" said
Mr Bear.

"Silly old Bear!
You gave us a scare!"
"Look at our tent!"
"The poles are bent!"

The little red plane went higher and higher ...

"OOOH! What a lovely view!" said Mr Bear.

Until ... PHUT!

The engine stopped!

"Hold tight!"
"Mummmmy!"
"My tummmmy!"
"Oh no! Down we go!"

At great speed the plane dived towards Hippo and her washing line.

106

"Watch how you go!"
"You'll hit Hippo!"
"Go over the top!"
"Oh, please! Can't
we stop!"
"LOOK OUT!"

SCRUMPH!

Mr Bear's first flight ended up in a tree!
"Wasn't that fun?" said Mr Bear.
"NO!" shouted all his friends.
But they didn't really mean it!

Little Piglet

Nicola Smee

Little Piglet has just been born.
He has lots of brothers and sisters.

Little Piglet has a curly tail and floppy ears,
and he likes to root around in the soil with
his pink snout.

He rushes around and squeals loudly,
but most of all Little Piglet likes his food!

When he's tired he flops down next to
Mother Pig. "Grunt!" she says to her Little
Piglet, "Grunt! Grunt!"

The Three Little Pigs

from The Orchard Book of Nursery Stories

Sophie Windham

Once upon a time there were three little pigs who went out into the world to seek their fortune.

The first little pig set off through the fields. He met a man carrying a bundle of straw.

"Please, man," said the little pig, "will you give me some straw so that I can build myself a house?"

"As much as you need, little pig," said he.

The man gave the straw to the little pig, and the little pig built himself a straw house.

In a little while a wolf came along and knocked on the door.

"Little pig, little pig," said the wolf, "let me come in."

"No, no, by the hair of my chinny, chin, chin, I will not let you in," said the little pig.

"Then I'll huff and I'll puff and I'll blow your house down," said the wolf.

And he huffed and he puffed and he blew the house down and ate up the little pig.

The second little pig went up the hill to the woods. There he met a man carrying a bundle of sticks.

"Please, man," said the little pig, "will you give me some sticks so that I can build myself a house?"

"As many as you need, little pig," said he.

The man gave some sticks to the little pig,

and the little pig built himself a wooden house.

In a little while the wolf came along and knocked on the door.

"Little pig, little pig," said the wolf, "let me come in."

"No, no, by the hair of my chinny, chin, chin, I will not let you in," said the little pig.

"Then I'll huff and I'll puff and I'll blow your house down," said the wolf.

And he huffed and he puffed and he blew the house down and ate up the second little pig.

The third little pig skipped down the lane towards the town. On the way he met a man carrying a load of bricks.

"Please, man," said the little pig, "will you give me some bricks so that I can build myself a house?"

"As many as you need, little pig," said he.

The man gave some bricks to the little pig, and the little pig built himself a brick house.

No sooner had the little pig settled into his new home than the wolf came along and knocked at the door.

"Little pig, little pig," said the wolf, "let me come in."

"No, no, by the hair of my chinny, chin, chin, I will not let you in," said the little pig.

"Then I'll huff and I'll puff and I'll blow your house down," said the wolf.

And he huffed and he puffed, and he puffed and he huffed, but he couldn't blow down the strong little brick house.

Then the wolf was angry. He sprang on to the roof and shouted, "Little pig, I'm coming down the chimney and I'm going to eat you up for my dinner!"

But the little pig was ready for the wolf. He had a big pot of water boiling on the fire, and he lifted the lid and the wolf fell right into the pot. Then the little pig slammed the lid on again, and that was the end of the wicked wolf.

And the little pig lived safe and snug in his little brick house for the rest of his life.

WELLIE BEAR

from Teddy Tales

Sally Grindley • Peter Utton

Wellie Bear wore smart red wellington boots and a bright blue plastic raincoat. But Wellie Bear wasn't a happy bear.

"Hrrmp! I'm fed up with being indoors," he moaned to himself. "I am a Wellie Bear.

I want to get wet. I want to jump in puddles. And I'm jolly well going to!"

The next day it began to pour with rain. When everyone had gone to bed and snores rumbled around the house, Wellie Bear tiptoed over to the window and climbed out on to the window ledge.

"It's raining, it's pouring,
They are all a'snoring,
And I'm going SPLASHING!"

With that, he slid down the drainpipe –
WHEE! – and landed with a bump
among the crocuses.

"I'm wet!" he shouted. "I've got a wet bottom and wet paws. Now for wet wellies!"

Wellie Bear stomped off down the path on a puddle hunt. The first puddle he came to was rather small, but that didn't matter to a bear who had never met a puddle before. He lifted one wellied foot up and – SPLASH!

– down it came into the puddle. He lifted the other wellied foot and – SPLASH! – down that one came into the puddle too.

Left SPLASH! right SPLASH! left
SPLASH! right SPLASH! left SPLASH!
right SPLASH!

"My wellies are wet, my wellies are wet!
That's what wellies are for!" yelled Wellie
Bear, at the top of his voice. "Now for a
bigger puddle."

Ten steps further on was a puddle that
made Wellie Bear's eyes water. He had never
seen such a huge puddle.

"Wow!" he shouted. "Count to three and
in I go. 1 – 2 – 3 – jump!"

And he leapt into the air and landed in the
puddle with a SPLASH! that soaked him
to the fur, and filled his wellies with water.
He got out of the puddle and jumped in
again – SPLASH! – and again – SPLASH!
A soggier bear you have never seen.

Wellie Bear was now very cold.
It was time to go home.
He squelched his way
back to the house.
But he couldn't
climb up the
drainpipe as easily
as he had slid down it.
It was far too slippery.

"What a silly bear
I am," he shivered,
"soaking wet,
freezing cold,
and stuck
out here."

He made his way round to the front of the house, crept under the doormat, and that's where he stayed until he was found the next morning.

"Perhaps I'll try the bath next time," thought Wellie Bear, as he hung out to dry on the clothes line, with his raincoat and wellies hanging alongside him.

Bathtime

Illustrated by Selina Young

Rub a dub dub,
Three babes in a tub
And who do you think got wet?
The daddy, the mummy,
The teddy bear's tummy,
So, hoppity, out you get!

Lucy Coats

The big ship sails on the alley alley oh,
The alley alley oh, the alley alley oh;
The big ship sails on the alley alley oh,
On the last day of September.

Plastic Penguin's Story

from Toybox Tales

Sally Grindley • Andy Ellis

Plastic Penguin was a bath toy. She used to stand on the edge of the bath waiting for Tom or Sarah to plunge her into the water. When they did she would whistle – PHHOOOO! – as the hot water flooded over her. It was always a shock, because penguins aren't used to hot water, even plastic penguins, but she loved being able to swim about.

When Tom and Sarah stopped playing with
her, Plastic Penguin was put into the toybox.
Sometimes they took her out just to look at her,
but they never put her in the bath again and
she really missed her swims.

One day Two Ton Ted shouted to all the toys,
"It's snowing! Come and look, it's snowing!"

The toys clambered out of the toybox as quickly
as they could and rushed to the window. They
peered out and saw great white flakes floating
past and falling slowly to the ground.

"PHOOOO!" whistled Plastic Penguin excitedly.
She had never seen snow before, but she knew
that snow was what real

penguins liked
more than
anything
else.

The other toys went back to the toybox and made themselves comfortable for the night. But Plastic Penguin watched and watched as the snow turned everything white. The garden didn't look like Tom and Sarah's garden any more. It looked like just the sort of place where even a plastic penguin would feel at home.

"Go and try it," said Two Ton Ted softly, "before it gets too dark. I'll watch out for you."

Plastic Penguin didn't need to be told twice. She waddled quietly out of the bedroom and down the stairs. She climbed through the cat flap, and there it was. Snow everywhere.

"PHHOOOO!" she whistled
as she stepped into it and the
snow covered her feet.
"It's cold! But it's what
penguins like best!"

She took a few more steps
and nearly fell over. Her feet slipped
and slid on the icy path – WHOOAAA!

Two Ton Ted chuckled from the bedroom
window. "What's it like?" he called.

"It's cold and it's slippery and it's crunchy,
and it's the most wonderful thing in the world!"
shouted Plastic Penguin. "Come down!"

"No, thanks," said Two Ton
Ted. "I like being in
the warm."

"Watch this then,"
said Plastic Penguin.
She took a few steps,
then she dropped on

129

to her tummy and tobogganed along the path – WHEEEEEEE! She stood up, turned round, and tobogganed back the other way – WHEEEEEEE! The third time, she went so fast that she couldn't stop.

"Look out!" yelled Two Ton Ted, but he was too late. Plastic Penguin whizzed off the garden path and straight into the pond – SPLASH! Then "PHHOOO!" she whistled, as the icy water flooded over her. It was a shock because plastic penguins aren't used to icy water.

"Are you all right?" called Two Ton Ted.

He needn't have worried. Plastic Penguin was swimming around and having the time of her life. Every now and again, she jumped out of the water and then plunged back in.

She swam on her front, she swam on her back, she twisted and turned and dived and leapt in the air – PHHOOOO! And then "PHOO!" she went, and "PH-", she was tired out. She dragged herself out of the pond and lay by the side, breathing heavily and shivering in the cold.

"What's the matter?" called Two Ton Ted.

Plastic Penguin didn't have enough strength to reply. Two Ton Ted rushed from the window, ran down the stairs, clambered through the downstairs window (he was too big to crawl through the cat flap) and began to make his way across the garden.

It wasn't easy. He slipped and slithered and fell head over heels. His paws grew heavier as the snow stuck to his fur. His whole body shook

with the cold. He tried tobogganing on his
tummy like Plastic Penguin, but he just spun
round in circles. So he crawled on his paws and
knees, until at last he reached his toybox friend.

"Come on, Plastic Penguin," he said. "Let's get
you back in the warm."

He took hold of her flipper and tried to
pull her along, but he kept falling over. So he
rolled her over on to her tummy, went back
down on his paws and knees, and pushed
her from behind.

When they reached the cat flap, Two Ton Ted lifted Plastic Penguin up and bundled her gently through the flap, then heaved himself in through the window.

By now, Two Ton Ted was tired out too. He knew he wouldn't be able to pull himself and Plastic Penguin back upstairs. So he carried her to the cat's basket, and that's where they spent the night.

Tom and Sarah never could understand how two of their toys came to be in the cat's basket. As for Plastic Penguin, she decided to wait for warmer weather before she went for another swim in the pond.

Little Chick

Nicola Smee

Little Chick has a strong little beak and is the first to break out of his egg.

He is tiny and damp but can soon run around. And he does!

Little Chick drinks water and eats corn and ruffles his fluffy yellow feathers.

At bedtime Little Chick snuggles up safe and warm under his mother's wing.

The Christmas Story

Nicola Smee

Mary and a carpenter called Joseph lived in the town of Nazareth.

One day Mary was surprised by the Angel Gabriel. He told her that she was going to have a baby and that the child would be the Son of God.

Some time later,
Mary and Joseph
travelled to Bethlehem.
All the inns were full,
so they had to stay in
a stable.

There, Mary
gave birth to
her son, Jesus.
She wrapped
Him up
warmly and
then laid Him
in a manger.

An Angel appeared to some
shepherds near by and told
them the good news.

They went and found the baby Jesus and knelt before Him in wonder. The shepherds were so excited they told everyone that they saw, and they were filled with wonder too.

Meanwhile, three wise men from the
East had seen a bright star and followed
it all the way to Bethlehem.

They brought gifts for the baby
Jesus and knelt before Him
for they knew He was
the Son of God.

Twinkle Twinkle

Selina Young

★

Twinkle, twinkle, little star,

How I wonder what you are.

Up above the world so high,

Like a diamond in the sky.

Twinkle, twinkle, little star,

How I wonder what you are.

★

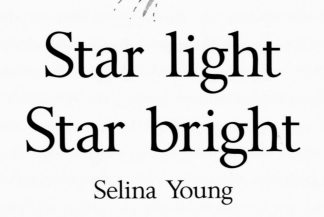

Star light
Star bright

Selina Young

★

Star light, star bright,

First star I see tonight,

I wish I may, I wish I might,

Have the wish I wish tonight.

★

THE EAR

This is a time when children really begin to explore books for themselves, an exciting time when firm favourites are established and requested over and over again.

As children begin to see themselves as readers they will pretend to read alone, reciting favourite storylines they have

LY YEARS

committed to heart, as they turn the pages of a book. These are the first steps on the path to reading.

The stories in this section have been chosen to stimulate discussion and laughter, as children use the situations they find in the stories to explore their own lives.

Billy and the Brilliant Babysitter

Hiawyn Oram • Sonia Holleyman

Billy's mother and father were going out. Billy didn't
like them going out. He specially didn't like them
going to a fancy dress ball.

His mother was going as Boadicea, the warrior queen.

His father was going as an American gangster
with a false gold tooth and a huge fake cigar.

Billy lay on the bed watching them putting the finishing touches to their costumes. He didn't need to close his eyes to see his father, with four other gangsters, driving to America. He didn't need to half-close his eyes to see his mother riding off into the hills.

He didn't need to breathe to see himself running after his father and then jumping on the running board of his gangster car and one of the gangsters pushing him off.

He didn't need to blink to see himself running after his mother and her chariot being too quick for him and disappearing, like a little blob, over the horizon ...

Billy rolled off the bed and lay on the carpet feeling absolutely, completely, one-hundred-percent certain that when his parents went out that night they were never coming back. Not ever.

He was terrified.

Then the doorbell rang. He knew who it was going to be.

It was going to be the new babysitter. He didn't want the new babysitter to come in because the moment she came in, his mother and father would go out.

He raced down the stairs to the front door.

"There's no one home!" he called through the letterbox. "Go away!"

But she didn't go away. She came right in. His father, the gangster, let her.

"Hey kid, how ya doin'?" he said in a silly voice. "Billy is shoor lookin' forward to meetin' ya."

"No he isn't," said Billy from the coat cupboard, "Billy's not here. You can go home."

"Of course he's here," said his mother, the warrior queen, swanning down the stairs and reaching into the cupboard. "He's here and he's going to be a good boy, isn't he?"

"No," said Billy, grabbing on to the warrior queen's knees and starting to scream.

The knees crossed the hall to the front door with Billy hanging on and screaming. "Don't go! Don't go! Don't go!" he screamed.

His father, the gangster, carried him back into the house. He put his fake cigar in his pocket and took off his hat.

"Now look, Bill, it's me, your dad, and we're only going to a party. We'll be back before you know it, chap, trust me."

But Billy wasn't sure he could

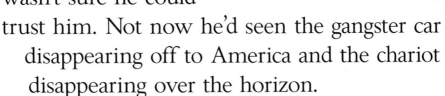

trust him. Not now he'd seen the gangster car disappearing off to America and the chariot disappearing over the horizon.

He tried to catch his father's coat tails through the door but before he could the new babysitter had picked him up. She

carried him upstairs and put
him into bed even though
he'd screamed and struggled
and kicked as hard as he
could to stop her.

Then she sat beside him
on the bed.

"Billy," she said, "I bet I
know what you're thinking. I bet
you're thinking your mother and father are going out,
not to a fancy dress ball. I bet you're thinking they're
going out and not coming back. Ever."

Billy stopped sobbing in amazement. How could
she know? No one else did. She must be brilliant.
She must be telepathic.

He turned to listen to more.

"I thought that, when I was little," she went on
telepathically. "But I was wrong. And you're wrong.

Why, right this minute, your mother and father are getting out of their car and walking up the path to the fancy dress ball behind a Big Brown Bear and a Goldilocks."

Billy didn't even need to close his eyes to see it.

"And now they're saying hello to Billy the Kid, not you of course, a grown up kid, and a fairy from the top of a Christmas tree and a can of Tomato Soup with legs."

Billy didn't even need to blink to see it.

"And now they're sitting down at a table with a Chess Piece and the Queen of Hearts, a Highwayman and a Bookworm. The Bookworm is leaning over to your mother and saying 'Pat, can Billy come to play on Saturday?'"

"That'll be my friend Joe's mother," said Billy, not needing to think twice to see it.

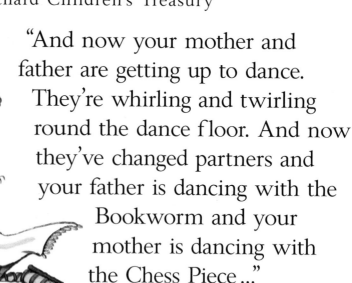

"And now your mother and father are getting up to dance. They're whirling and twirling round the dance floor. And now they've changed partners and your father is dancing with the Bookworm and your mother is dancing with the Chess Piece..."

"That'll be Joe's dad," said Billy. "He's chess-mad."

"And now they're having the most delicious supper with huge fluffy meringues and little sugar mice and marzipan frogs. Your mother is popping her sugar mice and marzipan frogs into her handbag to bring home to you. And your father is saying, as he always says about this time when they're out, 'We should be getting back to Billy soon...' and your mother is saying, 'I think I'll make a quick call to check he's all right...'"

Billy closed his eyes. He could just hear it. Besides, the telephone was ringing.

"Tell them, they can stay a bit longer," he said sleepily. "I'm O.K. here, I'm fine. Now I know where they are and as they're having such a good time."

"Sure," whispered the babysitter. "I'll tell them. And in the meantime, sleep well, Billy."

And he did.

And after that he never minded when his mother and father went out so long as he could have an even HALF brilliant, HALF telepathic babysitter who had SOME idea of what his parents were doing and when they were thinking of coming home... which, just like yours, they always were, and they always did.

Little Mouse Twitchy Whiskers

Margaret Mayo • Penny Dann

One day a little mouse called Twitchy Whiskers was running through the woods when she saw an old cardboard box. She stopped and twitched her whiskers.

"What's this – a warm house? It looks just right for a mouse!" she said.

She snuffled all around the box and twitched her whiskers again. Then she called out:

"Who lives in this house?"

But no one answered. So she crept inside.

After a while a frog came by, and when he saw the box, he called out:

"Who lives in this house?"

"Twitchy Whiskers lives here," said the little mouse. "And who are you?"

"I am the Croaking Frog," he said. "Please let me in."

"Come in," said Twitchy Whiskers. "Now we are two."

And so the frog hopped inside.

After a while a rabbit came by, and when he saw the box, he called out:

"Who lives in this house?"

"Twitchy Whiskers and the Croaking Frog live here," said the little mouse. "And who are you?"

"I am the Jumping Rabbit," he said. "Please let me in."

"Come in," said Twitchy Whiskers. "Now we are three."

And the rabbit jumped inside.

After a while a hen came by, and when she saw the box, she called out: "Who lives in this house?"

"Twitchy Whiskers and the Croaking Frog and the Jumping Rabbit live here," said the little mouse. "And who are you?"

"I am the Clucking Hen," she said. "Please let me in."

"Come in," said Twitchy Whiskers. "Now we are four."

And the hen bustled inside.

"Come in," said Twitchy Whiskers. "Now we are five."

And the duck waddled inside.

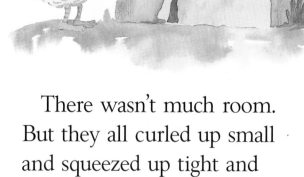

After a while a duck came by, and when she saw the box, she called out: "Who lives in this house?"

"Twitchy Whiskers and the Croaking Frog and the Jumping Rabbit and the Clucking Hen live here," said the little mouse. "And who are you?"

"I am the Waddling Duck," she said. "Please let me in."

There wasn't much room. But they all curled up small and squeezed up tight and somehow everyone fitted in.

Then a bear came by, and when he saw the box, he called out:

"Who lives in this house?"

"Twitchy Whiskers and the Croaking Frog and the Jumping Rabbit and the Clucking Hen and the Waddling Duck live here," said the little mouse. "And who are you?"

The bear said, "I am Bear Big-and-Fat who can squash you all flat, so LET ME IN!"

"I'm sorry," said Twitchy Whiskers. "But the house is full. We are curled up small and squeezed up tight and the house is stretched to bursting. So we cannot let you in."

The Bear growled, as loud as he could:

"Rumbling thunder! I'll tumble you under! This Bear Big-and-Fat will SQUASH YOU ALL FLAT!"

159

Then Twitchy Whiskers
and the frog and the rabbit
and the hen and the duck
opened their eyes very
wide, and they saw that
bear coming
down...
down...
down...
right on top of their house!

So out they tumbled
and off they ran, this
way and that way.
And the bear sat down
on the house – *WHUMPF!*
and he squashed
it all flat.

But he did *not* squash
Twitchy Whiskers and the
Croaking Frog and the
Jumping Rabbit and the
Clucking Hen and the
Waddling Duck. He
did *not* squash
them flat.

And they all got back to their own homes...
safe and sound.

Something Special

Nicola Moon   Alex Ayliffe

Friday was 'special' day in Mrs Brown's class. Everyone was allowed to bring in one of their favourite, special things to show the class.

"What can I take that's special?" asked Charlie one Friday morning. Mum was busy feeding Sally. "What about your teddy?" she said.

"Lots of people take their teddies," said Charlie. "I want to take something different."

Sally started crying. "Look in your bedroom," said Mum.

Charlie searched through his things. There was Bessie, the old rag doll from Africa that had belonged to his grandma. But she didn't look very special with her stuffing coming out.

There was the model boat he'd made all by himself. But it fell apart as soon as he tried to pick it up.

There was the beautiful chocolate rabbit he'd saved from Easter. But one ear had been bitten off.

"I can't find anything," said Charlie sadly. "Can you help me look?"

But Mum was busy dressing Sally.

"There's no time now," she said. "Don't look so miserable. We'll find something for you to take next week."

When they got to school the other children had lots of special things.

Raju had some sweet and sticky gulab jamun that smelt of rose petals, and he let everyone taste them.

Peter had a strange-looking plant called a 'Venus Fly Trap'. He said it ate flies and it would eat your finger if you weren't careful.

Lu Mei had a kite. It was made of bright red paper and shaped like a dragon. She said it came from China.

Charlie's best friend Steven brought in his pet hamster in a cage. Steven said its name was Biscuit and Joanne said it looked like a rat.

And Daniel had a huge slimy worm that he'd found on the way to school, but Mrs Brown made him put it outside.

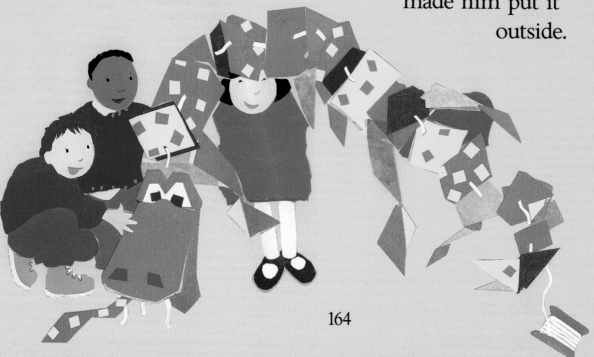

Shireen had a beautiful sari that sparkled blue and gold. She put it on and Mrs Brown said she looked like a princess.

But Charlie had nothing.

"Never mind," said Mrs Brown. "You can bring something next week."

"But I haven't got anything special," said Charlie on his way home. "Not special and different."

"What about your favourite book? Or Goldie the fish? Or your collection of postcards from Uncle Ali in Nigeria?" Mum said, trying hard to think of something.

"No, I don't want to take any of those," said Charlie.

When they got home Mum had to feed Sally again. And change her nappy. And wash her clothes. And put her to bed.

Charlie felt cross. He turned the television on really loud. He stamped around and slammed the door.

"Ssh! You'll wake your sister," said Mum.

"I don't care!" said Charlie to himself.

Charlie felt Mum would never have time to help him find something special.

On Saturday they had to go to the shops in the rain, because Mum had to buy more nappies for Sally.

On Sunday Auntie Jill and Uncle John came, and they made a big fuss of Sally all day.

On Monday they were late for school because Sally cried all night and they slept in.

On Tuesday Charlie went to Steven's house for tea. Steven had lots of special things. "You can borrow something if you like," he said. "But it wouldn't be mine," said Charlie.

On Wednesday Charlie felt very cross. He still couldn't think of anything special to take to school. And Sally was crying again.

Mum was busy making biscuits in the kitchen.

"You go to her," she said.

"I don't want to." Charlie stamped his foot and started to cry. "All she does is cry all the time and I haven't got anything that's special, nothing at all."

Mum took Charlie on to her knee.

"We'll find you something, you'll see. Now you go up and see Sally for me while I get the biscuits finished. Then you can have some warm from the oven, just how you like them."

Charlie went slowly up the stairs and into Sally's room. He covered his ears and looked at his sister. Her face was all screwed up like an angry prune and she was kicking her legs wildly in the air.

"Stupid babies," he muttered. He picked up one of Sally's baby toys and started to play with it. Sally stopped screaming.

Charlie looked into the cot. Sally looked at Charlie with her big brown eyes. Charlie looked at Sally. Her hands were so tiny!

He reached out and touched her fingers. She grabbed on to his finger so tightly he nearly cried out. But it felt nice. He didn't know babies were so strong.

"Hello, Sally," he said.

And then Sally did something she'd never done before. She smiled. A big beaming smile, just for Charlie.

Later that evening Mum came to tuck Charlie into bed. She held a wonderful carved wooden mask.

"I've found something for you to take to school," she said.

"But I've already got something," said Charlie, and whispered in Mum's ear.

At school on Thursday
Charlie was very excited.

"I'm bringing something
really special to show
tomorrow," he said.

"Is it a new toy?"
asked Lu Mei.

"No," said Charlie.

"Is it your goldfish?"
asked Steven.

"No," said Charlie.

"Is it something you
can eat?" asked Daniel.

"No," said Charlie.
"I'm not telling."

At last it was Friday.
The other children were
already waiting when
Mum brought Charlie
into the classroom.

"Charlie has something
special to show us this
morning," said Mrs Brown.

Today
is
Friday

"When will she be big
enough to play football?"
said Daniel.

"You are lucky,"
said Joanne.

"I wish I had
a baby sister,"
said Lu Mei.

"She isn't
smiling at me,"
said Steven.

"She only
smiles at me,"
said Charlie,
"because I'm
her brother."

"This is my baby sister,"
said Charlie proudly. "She's
called Sally and she's six
weeks old and she smiles
at me and she's very,
very special."

"She looks like you,"
said Peter.

That night Charlie helped Mum to bath Sally and put her to bed. "Do you know what special day it will be tomorrow?" asked Mum when Sally was asleep. "No," said Charlie.

"It's going to be Big Brother Day," said Mum. "A special day for big brothers, because big brothers really are 'something special'."

Poems from
Rumble in the Jungle
Giles Andreae   David Wojtowycz

Giraffe

Some animals laugh
At the gangly giraffe
But I hold my head up and feel proud,
I really don't care
When my head's in the air
And my cheek's getting kissed by a cloud.

Hippopotamus

Hello, I'm a big happy hippo
I sleep in the sun to get hot,
And when I'm not sleeping
I mooch in the mud,
Which hippos like doing a lot.

Zebra

I could have been grey like a donkey
Or brown like my cousin the mule,
But instead I've got stripes
Which my ladyfriend likes,
As they make me look handsome and cool.

Leopard

If you meet a hungry leopard
Prowling through the night,
Make sure you call him 'Sir'
And be incredibly polite.

Little Blue Car

Gwen Grant

Susan Hellard

Once upon a time, there was a factory that made cars. Red cars, yellow cars, black cars and green cars, pink cars and one little blue car.

When the little blue car had been made, he was put outside to sit in the sunshine.

"I am so warm," sighed the little blue car. "I wish I could go to the seaside."

He looked at the gate. Through the gate he could see a road. "I'm going," he said.

And the little blue car ran down the road to the sea.

The little blue car stayed in the sea all day. He didn't notice it was getting dark. Then it started to get cold and his tyres were frozen.

"Brrrrr!" he shivered. "I think I'll come out now."

When he got on to the sand, he saw that everyone else had gone.

"I don't like the seaside any more!" he cried. "I want to go home!"

The little blue car drove away and left the seaside far behind.

"It's very dark," he whispered. "I can't see where I'm going." Then he stopped. He was too scared to go any further.

"Of course you've got lights. Press that switch just there." The little blue car pressed the switch, and on came all his lights.

"Goodbye," said the bus, as he trundled away.

The little blue car wasn't frightened any more. He had his lights on.

But now he was tired.

"Ohhhhh," he yawned, and his bonnet opened as wide as it could go.

Then he saw a sign. LAYBY, the sign said.

Over the hill came a big red bus with all its lights on.

"What are you doing here?" asked the bus.

"I'm lost," said the little blue car. He was very unhappy.

"Why don't you put your lights on and then you'll know where you are?" the bus said.

"Have I got lights?"

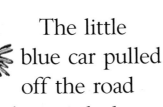

The little blue car pulled off the road into the dark quiet layby.

There were trees in the layby. There were owls and foxes with shining eyes.

"Who are you?" the owls asked.

But the little blue car was fast asleep.

When he woke up in the morning, he was frozen stiff. His whole body was white with frost.

"Oh!" he cried. "I'm freezing! I don't like the layby any more!" the little blue car wailed. "I want to go home!"

Down the road came an enormous lorry. The lorry stopped when it saw the little blue car.

"BLAAR, BLAAAR!" hooted the lorry. "You look very cold."

"I am cold," the little blue car said.

"Well, why don't you switch your heater on and get warm?" the lorry asked.

179

"Have I got a heater?"

"Of course you've got a heater. Press that switch just there."

The little blue car pressed the switch. On came the heater. The heater made him warm.

"Goodbye," the lorry hooted, and roared away.

The little blue car wasn't frightened any more. He had his lights on. He had his heater on. He drove down the wide road. But he was tired of moving. He wanted to play.

Then he saw a field and the little blue car ran straight on to the grass.

The grass tickled his tyres. Lambs played and jumped all round him. They looked through his windows.

"What are you?" the lambs asked.

"I'm a little blue car," he said.

The little blue car played in the field all morning. He didn't notice the sun had gone. Then he heard a noise on his roof. Pitter patter, pitter patter, pitter patter pit.

"Whatever's that?" he said.

He drove across the field. Then he stopped. He couldn't see through the water on his windscreen.

"I don't like this field any more!" the little blue car cried. "I want to go home!"

Over the field came a bright shiny tractor with all its lights on.

"Toot, toot, toot! You look very wet," the tractor piped.

"I am wet," said the little blue car. "And I can't see a thing."

"Why don't you put your windscreen wipers on, so you can see where you're going?" the tractor asked.

"Have I got windscreen wipers?" asked the little blue car.

"Of course you've got windscreen wipers. Press that switch just there."

The little blue car pressed the switch and on came his windscreen wipers. Swish swish. Swish swish.

"Goodbye, goodbye," and the tractor rumbled away.

The little blue car wasn't frightened any more. He had his lights on. He had his heater on and he had his windscreen wipers on.

The little blue car drove out of the field. The rain stopped and the sun began to shine.

He drove straight down the road, all the way back to the factory. He drove straight in through the factory gates.

He could see all the other cars. And, best of all, he could see his very own parking space.

"Hooray!" said the little blue car. "I'm home at last!"

CHARLIE'S CHOICE

NICOLA SMEE

One Saturday morning Grandpa invited Charlie to
   stay for the night.
   "Thanks, Grandpa, I'd like that!" said Charlie.
   Charlie ran upstairs to pack.
   "You don't need to take too much," said Mum. "And
just take *one* of your toys."
   The toys all wondered which one of them he'd take.
But not for long...

Mr Monkey had decided.

"Charlie's sure to pick me. After all, I am the one who takes him on adventures, and this will certainly be an adventure!"

"But I'm his Big Blue Bear and we growl at each other and feed each other spoonfuls of honey. Charlie can't do without me, not even for one day – he told me so!" said Big Blue Bear.

"I'm afraid you're both going to be disappointed then," said Tiger Puppet. "Charlie's bound to take me. We're very good at entertaining people and Grandpa likes a good laugh, I've heard him!"

"There's no way I'll be left behind!" said Percy Penguin. "I join Charlie in the bath every night and make sure he's clean. His mum says I do a good job!"

The toys started squabbling. Each thought they
would be needed more than the other, so it
was some time before they noticed
Little Mouse squeaking in the
background.

"What about me?
What about me!"

"You!" laughed all the other toys. "Why on earth should Charlie choose you, Little Mouse? Your job is the least important, if you can even call it a job!"

Charlie looked at his toys and thought long and hard.

He loved them all and he loved visiting Grandpa, but this time he was staying ALL NIGHT in the SPARE ROOM!

"Get a move on, Charlie," Mum shouted up the stairs. "Grandpa's here!"

Charlie had decided...

Little Mouse's job of
sleeping on Charlie's pillow
was important after all!

Mr Bear to the Rescue

Debi Gliori

It was a wild and windy night in the forest. The kind of night where the best place to be was in bed, snug and warm, with windows and doors tightly shut to keep the weather out.

Mr Bear was tucked up in bed, while outside the wind was shaking the windows and howling down the chimney, trying to get in.

"What was that noise?" said Mrs Bear, sitting up.

"Just the wind, dear," said Mr Bear.

"I thought I heard a voice calling *Help!*" said Mrs Bear.

"Help!" said a small voice.

"There," said Mrs Bear. "I did hear a voice. Go and see who it is, dear."

192

Mr Rabbit-Bunn.

"Our warren has collapsed," he wailed. "The Hoot-Toowits' nest has blown away, the Buzzes' hive is ruined and I have to go back because we can't find baby Flora *anywhere*," said Mr Rabbit-Bunn, and ran off into the night.

"Help is on its way," said Mr Bear, lighting a lantern, packing his tools and grabbing a honey sandwich, just in case.

Mr Bear obediently went downstairs. As he opened the front door, a blast of wind blew out his candle and peppered him with fallen leaves.

"Please help," said a very small voice from somewhere around Mr Bear's ankles.

Clinging on tight to Mr Bear's doorstep was

"Do be careful, dear," called Mrs Bear, as Mr Bear was blown down the garden path.

"Don't worry," said Mr Bear, feeling very worried indeed. "I'll be fine."

It was a long way to
the Rabbit-Bunns' house.
Mr Bear tripped and
stumbled over fallen
branches and several
times his lantern
nearly blew
out.

"I wish I was back
in my warm bed,"
thought Mr Bear.
Icy rain blew into
his face as he struggled
up the hill. "Just a little
further," said Mr Bear to
encourage himself.

A tangle of feathers and claws blew into Mr Bear's face. "Aaaaargh!" he shrieked.

"Eeeek!" squawked Mr Hoot-Toowit.

"Oh, it's *you!*" they both cried in unison.

Mr Bear struggled to his feet and peered into the darkness.

"I can't see your house anywhere," he said.

"You're standing in it," said Mr Hoot-Toowit sadly.

"Goodness, so I am," said Mr Bear.

There, all around, lay the battered remains of the tree that Mr Hoot-Toowit had shared with his family, the Buzz family, and the Rabbit-Bunns.

"Oh, Mr Bear, thank heavens you've come!" cried a voice.

"Can you help us find Flora?"

"And can you fix our hive?"

"And mend our nest?"

Mr Bear was instantly surrounded by rabbits and owls and bees, all beseeching him for help.

"Help!" thought Mr Bear. "What on earth am I supposed to do?"

He scrabbled around in his tool-kit and found the honey sandwich that he'd thrown in there as he left his house. A brilliant idea occurred to him.

"What's that for?" asked one of the small Rabbit-Bunns.

"Glue," said Mr Bear, peeling the sandwich apart. "Hive-glue, in fact. Look, I'll spread a little bit here and another dollop there and … "

"End up with a sticky mess," groaned a small Buzz.

"Oh dear," said Mr Bear. "Let's take the hive home for Mrs Bear to fix. She's very good at that sort of thing."

"What about my nest?" said Mr Hoot-Toowit.

"I'll just have a look," said Mr Bear, picking it up. The nest fell apart in his paws. Mrs Hoot-Toowit sighed.

"Ah," said Mr Bear. "Mrs Bear will knit you another one in no time."

As the animals put the sticky hive and broken nest into Mr Bear's tool-kit, the heavens opened.

Rain poured down through the trees, seeking out anything that was dry and turning it instantly cold and soggy.

The animals all ran for shelter.

Mr Bear's lantern hissed, fizzled and went out.

"How will we ever find

Flora now?" wailed Mrs Rabbit-Bunn.

Mr Bear looked up at the sky anxiously.

"Good grief," he said.

"What's that?" said Mr Hoot-Toowit through a mouthful of twigs.

"I've found Flora!" yelled Mr Bear, pointing upwards.

There, high in the branches of the sheltering tree, was a small rabbit, still wrapped in a blanket and fast asleep.

"I'll just climb up there and get her," said Mr Bear.

"What a hero you are," sighed Mrs Rabbit-Bunn.

Mr Bear didn't feel heroic as he inched up the tree.

The slippy rain-soaked branches gave out alarming groans and creaks as he grabbed them.

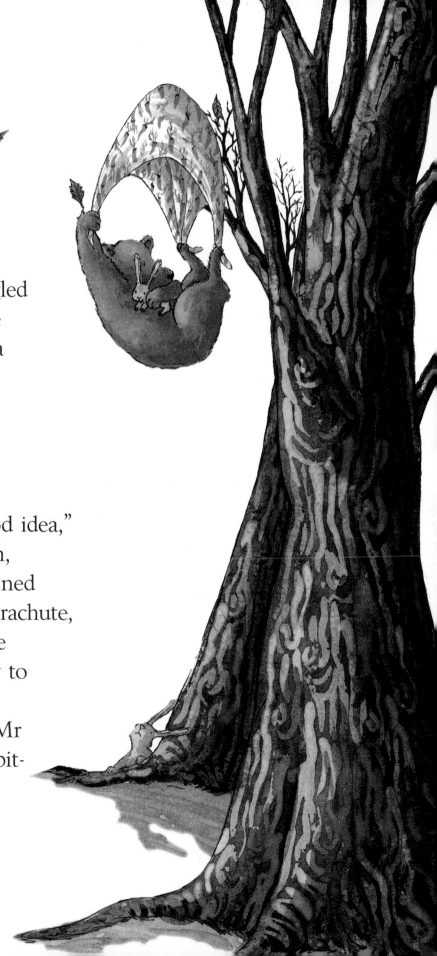

Mr Bear disentangled
the blanket from the
branch, cradled Flora
in his arms and ...
"Aaaargh!" yelled
Mr Bear.

"Wheeeeee!" said
Flora, waking up.

"Gosh, what a good idea,"
said Mr Rabbit-Bunn,
as Flora's blanket fanned
out into a perfect parachute,
and Mr Bear and the
bunny floated safely to
the ground.

"What a brilliant Mr
Bear!" said Mrs Rabbit-
Bunn, rushing over
and hugging Mr
Bear's knees.

"Let's get these children tucked up in bed," said
Mr Bear, loading the Rabbit-Bunns, Buzzes and
Hoot-Toowits into his tool-kit.
"It's very dark," said Mr Hoot-Toowit.
"I can't see!" wailed a small Rabbit-Bunn.

"Neither can I," thought Mr Bear,
pushing his laden tool-kit to the top of a
hill. But there, off in the distance, was his
house with all the lights on, shining
through the darkness.

"Hold on tight," he said.
"We're nearly home."

And much later, when towels and blankets had been found for everyone, and Mrs Bear's hot nettle soup had warmed every tummy, the Bear house filled with snores.

Baby Bear clambered up Mr Bear's leg. Mr Bear sank into a chair with a groan.

Mrs Bear looked up from her nest-knitting.

"What a brilliant Mr Bear your daddy is," she said. "So good at fixing things."

Mr Bear gave a huge yawn. "In fact," continued Mrs Bear, "there are a few things

round here that could do with being fixed by that daddy. There's the squeaky door, the blocked sink and the smoky chimney ..."

Mr Bear gave a loud snore. "... but they can all wait till tomorrow," said Mrs Bear, fetching a warm blanket.

"Even brilliant Mr Bears need to be tucked in at times," she said, as she blew out the candles and headed upstairs to bed.

Katie and the Dinosaurs

James Mayhew

"Come and look, Grandma, come and see the dinosaurs!" said Katie.

Katie loved the natural history museum, and she wanted to show her Grandma everything.

"They're just a load of old bones," said Grandma.

"Well, you're really old," said Katie. "There must have been dinosaurs alive when you were little."

"I'm not that old!" snorted Grandma, looking for somewhere to sit down. "Why don't you go and look at your horrible dinosaurs while I have forty winks," she said.

"They're not horrible," sniffed Katie. "But I do wish they weren't just skeletons." And she skipped off on her own, taking her picnic lunch with her, just in case.

Katie saw spiky dinosaurs, fishy dinosaurs, flying dinosaurs, horned dinosaurs, long dinosaurs ...

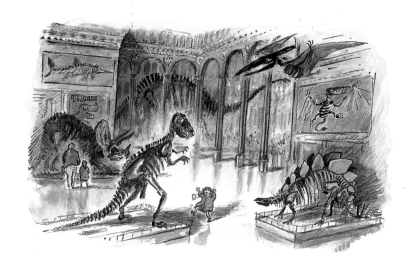

She closed her eyes and tried to imagine they were alive. She thought they must have been very frightening with their sharp teeth and claws.

Next to one of the dinosaurs was a corridor. Katie set off down it to make sure that she hadn't missed anything worth seeing.

The corridor was long and dark, and there was no one in sight. Katie began to feel scared. She looked for a 'Way Out' sign, but there didn't seem to be one. She was lost.

"Now what do I do?" said Katie crossly.

She came to a big door with a notice on it that said:

ABSOLUTELY
NO ADMITTANCE
WHATSOEVER

"I'll just take a quick look," said Katie and she opened the door and stepped through.

The door led outside and there in front of her was a dinosaur! It was no bigger than Katie, but it was a real live one!

"Hello," said Katie. "Who are you?"

"Hadrosaurus," said the dinosaur. "Who are *you*?"

"I'm Katie," said Katie, "and I think I'm lost."

"I'm lost too," said Hadrosaurus. "I was chased by a Tyrannosaurus Rex."

"Isn't that the really fierce dinosaur?" asked Katie.

"That's right," said Hadrosaurus. "Now I don't know how to get home."

"Don't worry," said Katie. "I'll be able to see where we are from the top of this hill," and she clambered up a steep slope.

"This isn't a hill!" said Hadrosaurus, scrambling up behind her.

Katie gasped. "Oh, it's a brontosaurus!" She was very high up and she could see for miles.

"Now show me where you live," said Katie.

"I think it's somewhere over there, along the river bank," said Hadrosaurus.

Katie looked across the river.

"What are those funny-looking birds?" she asked.

"They're Pterosaurs," said Hadrosaurus. "Watch out!"

But one of the Pterosaurs had already spotted Katie's yellow scarf. It swooped towards her and before Katie could duck, it had snatched the scarf from her.

"Hey, that's mine! Bring it back!" yelled Katie.

But the Pterosaur was far away already.

Now the Brontosaur started to move. She was getting fed up with those two noisy creatures jumping about on her back. How they made her itch!

Katie hung on for dear life, slipping and sliding about on the Brontosaurus's back as she lumbered down to the river for a nice cool bathe. She was so huge that Katie and Hadrosaurus hardly got wet at all.

From high up on the Brontosaurus's back Katie could look right out to sea. All sorts of strange creatures were swimming there. She recognised some of them from the museum - the Ichthyosaurs with their long snouts, and a Plesiosaur with its snake-like neck.

Before long the Brontosaurus reached the shore.

"Let's go," said Katie. Followed by Hadrosaurus, she slid all the way down to the tip of the Brontosaurus's tail and they landed in a giggling heap on the ground.

The Brontosaurus chuckled a deep thundery laugh.

"Which way now?" said Katie.

"Into the jungle," said Hadrosaurus.

The jungle was hot and sticky. Katie could see a herd of enormous dinosaurs.

"What are those?" asked Katie. "I don't like the look of *them*."

"Only Stegasaurs," said Hadrosaurus. "They won't hurt us."

"Are you sure?" said Katie suspiciously, as one Stegasaur licked its lips.

"Oh yes, they only eat plants," said Hadrosaurus. So Katie gave them some grass. Then they went through the jungle and soon the trees began to thin out.

Suddenly Hadrosaurus let out a squeal! "Mama! Papa!" It was Hadrosaurus's family.

His mama and papa hugged him and hugged Katie too for bringing him home.

"I hope you're not going to eat me," worried Katie.

"Don't be afraid, Katie," said Hadrosaurus, "we only eat plants too."

That reminded Katie that she hadn't had her picnic lunch yet. She was feeling quite hungry by now.

Katie politely shared her cucumber sandwiches and chocolate biscuits. She saved her meat pie for later.

Plant-eating dinosaurs from far and wide picked up the smell of Katie's sandwiches, and padded across the rocks towards her.

There was a Styracosaurus and a Triceratops with their horns, an Iguanodon with his spiky thumbs and some Ankylosaurs.

The dinosaurs shook some strange-looking fruits out of the trees and they all ate until they were full.

It was the best picnic Katie had ever had.

Suddenly, another dinosaur crashed out of the jungle. It was Tyrannosaurus Rex! He had been following Katie and Hadrosaurus all along.

He grunted and growled and ground his teeth, and swished his tail and stamped his scaly feet. He was hungry! And he didn't want cucumber sandwiches or chocolate biscuits, he wanted meat! He wanted Katie!

"Quick, run for your life!" said Hadrosaurus, and Katie took to her heels.

All the dinosaurs ran away in alarm.

Tyrannosaurus Rex thundered after Katie and the dinosaurs as they ran through the jungle towards the river.

Katie got out of breath, but she kept on running.

At last she could see the museum ahead of her. If only she had stayed safely inside!

Then she remembered the meat pie. She tore open her lunch box and threw a piece at the Tyrannosaurus Rex.

The Tyrannosaurus stopped in his tracks. He sniffed the piece of pie. He ate it up. He liked it so much that Katie threw him the rest, even though she had been saving it for herself.

And the Tyrannosaurus Rex padded off into the jungle again, contentedly clutching Katie's lunch box.

"Whew! That was close!" said Katie.

It was getting late now so Katie turned to say goodbye to Hadrosaurus.

"I do wish you could come home with me," she said, "but Grandma would only scream and make a fuss,"

"I'm happy here with my family anyway," said Hadrosaurus. "Thank you for helping me find them."

He gave Katie a lick.

"BLEAGH!" spluttered Katie, as dinosaurs have very sloppy tongues. Then she went back through the door into the museum.

This time Katie easily found her way through the museum. Grandma was waiting where she had left her.

"Where on earth have you been?" asked Grandma.

"I've seen all kinds of dinosaurs," said Katie. "Why don't you come and have a look too?"

"All right," said Grandma. "Where do we start?"

"This way," said Katie, taking her hand, and off they went.

The Smallest Whale

 Elisabeth Beresford   Susan Field

One sunny day a family of whales were swimming along in the deep blue sea. Right at the end came the Smallest Whale. He wasn't supposed to be at the end. He should have been right in the middle near his mother, but he kept turning to the left and to the right and diving down deep.

The Smallest Whale's mother had the rest of her family to look after and keep in line. She did this by singing to them on a very high note. The sound went up and down, up and down.

"WHEEWHAA WHEEWHAA..." she went, which means 'follow me'.

But soon the Smallest Whale had fallen so far behind the other whales that he was now closer to a fishing boat than he was to his mother.

"WHEEWHAAWHEE WHAA..." heard the Smallest Whale and he turned and began to follow the fishing boat. It was much the same size as his mother and it was making very nearly the same calling cry.

The boat came chugging into the harbour and the Smallest Whale went along with it.

Josh leaned over the back of the boat. "Dad!" he shouted. "There's an enormous whale following us!"

The poor little whale didn't know what had happened. He just lay there with his sides heaving. He was very, very frightened. There was no familiar call from his mother and there was no comforting water around him.

"Come on, Dad!" said Josh. "We've got to help him."

"We'd only hurt him if we tried to move him," said his father. "But he'll dry out and die if we leave him till the next high tide."

"Watch out!" shouted his father. "It's going to overturn us!" He turned the boat and the Smallest Whale – who did look enormous to Josh – went swimming past.

The Smallest Whale was going so fast he couldn't stop himself and the next moment he had swum right on to the pebble beach. Scrunch!

"Then we'll have to keep him wet," said Josh.

"Perhaps the fire brigade could help?" said his father.

"I'll go and tell them," said Josh. "And I'll get all my friends to help." Then he leaned close to the Smallest Whale. "Don't worry, we'll help you."

The Smallest Whale could just hear Josh's voice.

His sides heaved even more as he tried to make a sound himself. But none came out. There was nothing he could do but lie there and flip his tail in the water as the sea rippled away from him.

"There's an enormous whale on the beach. Everyone get a bucket or a can and get down there. We've got to keep him wet or he'll die. Hurry. Hurry. Hurry."

"Emergency! Stranded whale on the beach..." shouted Josh, and he ran up the high street as fast as he could. "Emergency! Emergency!" he shouted again as he dashed into the playground.

Meanwhile, back on the beach the Smallest Whale was gasping and making little clicking noises for his mother. And out in the sea his mother was calling for him: "WHEEWHAAWHEE WHAA!" But the sound would only travel through water and the Smallest Whale couldn't hear it.

people from the village.

The firemen rattled down the beach and into the water with the hose. And everyone else from the village made a line into the sea and got ready with their buckets and bowls. And when everyone was ready Josh shouted, "One, two, three ... WHOOSH!"

The Smallest Whale felt a wonderful splash of cold water. And then another. With every splash he felt better, but he was still too weak to open his eyes.

The Smallest Whale didn't hear the fire engine arrive with all the crew. Nor did he hear Josh close behind, running up with all his friends and all the

went to work even faster than before.

Whoosh! Whoosh! And again, Whoosh!

Very fuzzily the Smallest Whale heard the children's high voices all around him. Their shouting almost sounded like "WHEE WHAAWHEEWHAA..."

That couldn't be his mother, could it? As a little ripple of water touched his tail, the Smallest Whale flicked it feebly.

Whoosh! Whoosh! And again, Whoosh! It was very hard work for the rescuers.

Josh's father stopped to wipe his forehead. "I don't know whether he's going to last until the tide comes in again," he said.

"He's not going to dry out!" shouted Josh. "He's not. He's not! We're going to save the whale."

"Save the whale!" cried all the children and they

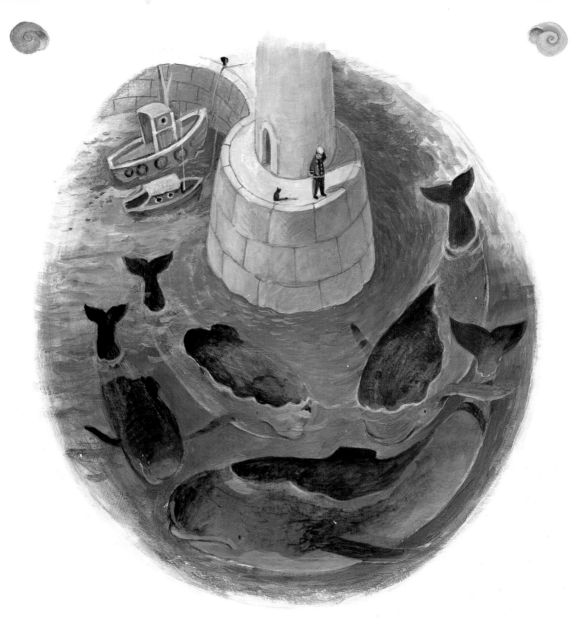

The Smallest Whale's mother was not so very far away. "WHEEWHAA WHEEWHAA!" she sang, as the whales swam backwards and forwards outside the harbour wall.

Back on the beach the Smallest Whale lay still.

But the tide was coming in and with each ripple of water he felt a little better.

"We'd better give him a helping hand with the boat," said Josh's father.

"WHEEWHAAWHEE WHAA..." The engine started up and slowly Josh's father turned the boat round and backed towards the beach.

Josh and the children went on pouring water onto the whale's shiny black back. Whoosh! Whoosh! And again, Whoosh!

The tide was coming in faster now. The fireman began to wind a thick rope around the Smallest Whale. And a big wave rolled in, Whoosh!

This time it was the Smallest Whale whooshing as the sea rocked him.

Josh's father quickly fastened the rope to the boat and then lifted Josh on board.

Splash! Another big wave came rolling in. The Smallest Whale floated for a few seconds. He felt wonderful! His own weight had been crushing his body. Then the next big wave came rolling in and it lifted the Smallest Whale clean off the pebbles.

strength as the engine of the fishing boat spluttered and whirred.

Suddenly the Smallest Whale was on the move. Everyone on the beach cheered and jumped up and down. The Smallest Whale managed to open his eyes and he made a very small "WHEEWHAAWHEE WHAA!" sound.

"One, two, three," called Josh's father.

And everyone on the beach pushed with all their

And out at sea all his family called back to him. "WHEEWHAAWHEE WHAA..."

Yes, *that* was the sound he really knew! Not the wheezy old sound of the fishing boat engine.

Suddenly the smallest whale put his head down under the waves and dived as hard as he could.

"Whoa!" shouted Josh's father and just in time he managed to slip the rope.

The Smallest Whale dived down, down, deep, down into the familiar cool sea. And he swam fast, faster than he had ever swum before, towards his mother.

"WHEEWHAAWHEE WHAA," he called to her.

"WHEEWHAAWHEE WHAA," his mother sang back to him.

Back on the beach
the villagers watched
the Smallest Whale, far
out to sea now, flick
his tail and join the rest
of his happy family.

And if Josh and his
friends and the people
of the village had listened
very carefully they might
just have heard the Smallest
Whale singing to them,
"Thank you for saving
my life."

"WHEEEWHAAAWHEEEWHAAA..."

A Balloon for Grandad

Nigel Gray ▲ Jane Ray

It was a warm day so the back door stood wide open.
Sam's balloon snuggled up against the ceiling. It was
bobbing and bumping
in the breeze.

After breakfast,
Sam and Dad
went upstairs to
wash their hands.

From the bathroom window Dad caught sight of a glint of silver and red.

"Look! There goes your balloon," he said. "It must have blown out of the back door!" They watched it rising up as straight and smooth as a lift on its way to the very top floor of a building taller than the tallest tree.

They went downstairs and went outside. Up and up went the balloon, jerkily, fidgety now, in fits and starts like a rock climber zig-zagging up a cliff.

And then, the wind grabbed it.
"I want my balloon," Sam cried.
"No!" said the wind.
"It's mine! All mine!"
And off rushed the
balloon, in a hurry now,
towards the mountains.

"Don't cry," said Dad.
"Across the mountains
is the sea, and across
the sea is the desert,
and across the desert,
a river, and in the
river, an island."

"And on that island," said Sam, "my grandad Abdulla lives, tending his goats."

"That's right," said Dad.

"Perhaps," said Sam, "my balloon is going to visit Grandad Abdulla."

"Yes," said Dad.

"Then it will fly high, high, high over the snow-decorated mountains where golden eagles nest...

high, high over the sparkling blue-green sea where silver fish leap from the waves...

high over the hot yellow sand of the desert where scorpions, and spitting spiders, and sidewinder snakes hide from the heat."

"And sand grouse
will peck at it," said
Sam, "and falcons will
fall on it, and hawks
will fly after it, and
vultures with their big
hooky beaks and their sharp
talons will tear at it, but the
dry desert wind will help it
dodge and weave and
nothing will harm it."

"That's right," said
Dad. "And then, tired
after its long journey,
it will see down below
the long blue ribbon of
the river; it will see the
small gold and emerald
jewel of the island;
it will see the little
brown house built
of baked mud.

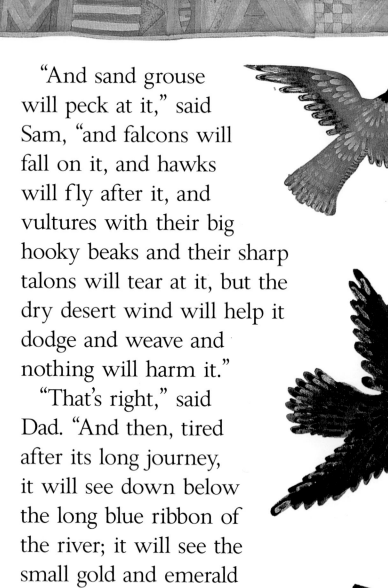

"Yes," said Sam, "and it will see Grandad Abdulla sitting in the shade of his mango tree. And down, down, down it will glide, landing in the yard like a seagull settling on the sea.

And Grandad Abdulla will say, 'A balloon! A balloon for me! My grandson Sam must have sent it to show that, although he's so far away, he's thinking of me'."

"Yes. It's sad to see it go," said Dad, "but the balloon will be happy after its great adventure. And Grandad Abdulla will be happy thinking of you."

"I'm glad my balloon's gone to see Grandad,"
said Sam, "because if I know Grandad's happy,
then I feel happy too."

FINDERS KEEPERS

From Counting Leopard's Spots

Hiawyn Oram • Tim Warnes

The Tortoises' hard work in their garden had borne fruit; pumpkins, pineapples and lots of sweet potatoes.

But Mrs Tortoise wasn't satisfied. "Oh, for a change of diet," she sighed. "Oh, for a bag of corn."

"If it's corn you want, my dear," Tortoise said generously, "then corn is what you shall have. I'll take some of our produce to market and exchange it for a bag of corn."

So though it was hot and he didn't feel like it, Tortoise placed two pumpkins, two pineapples and lots of sweet potatoes in a basket, balanced it on his back and set off.

The basket was heavy. The way was long. The sun had no mercy. Suddenly, Tortoise heard the inviting babble of a stream. He couldn't resist. He put the basket down on the hot path and clambered through the undergrowth for a long, cool, drink.

But while he was refreshing himself, who should come down the path but Monkey.

"Goodness gracious!" she cried, seeing the basket lying unattended. "It must be my birthday!"

And with a very naughty chuckle she picked it up, placed it over her arm and sauntered off into the shade to begin her feast.

Tortoise, returning from the stream, was beside himself. "It can't be!" he cried. "It was right here and now it's not. And no one would be so mean as to take it...?"

"Wouldn't they?" Butterfly, who had witnessed the whole scene, fluttered over. "Then take a look there in the shade."

Tortoise looked and could hardly believe what he saw.

Greedily and wastefully, Monkey had taken bites out of several potatoes and was already halfway through a pumpkin.

"Stop that at once!" Tortoise shouted. "That basket and all that is in it is mine!"

"Sorry," Monkey grinned, "but I don't know what you're talking about. I found this basket lying unattended on the path."

"That's because I put it there in order to go and take a drink from the stream!" Tortoise yelled.

"And if you won't give it back to me this minute, I'll take my case to Elephant."

"Then do that," said Monkey, spitting pumpkin pips cheerfully. "Because I know the law around here even if you don't, and it's 'finders keepers' on the beaten path."

But Tortoise was not so hot under the shell that he wasn't listening.

Elephant was holding court that evening and, determined to get justice, Tortoise presented his case. Butterfly supported it. So did Lizard who'd also seen the whole thing.

But Monkey was unrepentant. "There is no case," she said, swinging in with the basket on her arm and a whole troop of relatives to support her. "The basket was lying unattended on the beaten path. I found it. I keep it. Tell me that isn't the law."

Elephant shuffled and muttered into his trunk. "Unfortunately," he trumpeted softly, "Monkey is right. 'Finders keepers' IS the law in these parts. As much as it pains me, Tortoise – for I know how much work you and your wife put into your garden – Monkey keeps the basket and all that's in it."

Then Monkey and her relatives screeched with delight and scampered off, leaving Tortoise deeply dejected at what he felt was a terrible injustice.

However, it was not in Tortoise's nature to stay low for long.

"I tell you what, my dear," he said to Mrs Tortoise. "I'll go and visit my brother and see if he can spare a few cobs of corn to cheer us up."

And so the next morning Tortoise set out along the path that led to his brother's. As always the way was long and the sun was hot. He was just thinking of taking a short rest when he saw something ahead of him which made his heart miss a beat.

Surely it isn't, he reasoned with himself. Surely it can't be...

But he crept closer and saw that it was. Monkey – no doubt stuffed with sweet potatoes, pumpkin and pineapple – was fast asleep on the side of the path. Her tail, however, lay on the path.

The sight made Tortoise dizzy with excitement.

"I'll show you the law!" he cried dizzily. "And how to uphold it!" And without further ado, he clamped Monkey's tail hard in his mouth and began to move off.

"Hey! Stop! Stop thief! What are you doing with my tail?" Monkey screeched.

Luckily for Tortoise who couldn't open his mouth to answer, at that moment, Butterfly chanced along. "Looks to me, Monkey, as if Tortoise found your tail lying on the path and is keeping it," she laughed.

"Looks like that to me too." Even luckier for
Tortoise, Elephant emerged from a thicket. "Of
course," he trumpeted, "you are welcome to bring
your case to court, Monkey. But I can tell you
now, you'll be wasting your time. For in this case,
as in the basket case, finders will be keepers. So
go ahead, Tortoise, bite it off and take it home to
your wife for a fly whisk."

"Nooooo! No! Please!" Monkey screeched.
"Not my precious tail. Not a fly whisk. Anything
but that. Look, listen, give me back my tail and
I'll give you back your basket, and I'll give you a
bag of sweet potatoes!"

"Not enough," Elephant trumpeted. "Not for saving a tail from becoming a fly whisk. The basket, a bag of sweet potatoes and a bag of corn! By tomorrow afternoon."

Then very sulkily Monkey agreed – what choice did she have?

And, smiling quietly to himself, Tortoise let go of her tail, thanked Elephant profoundly and made his way home.

And though supper that night was still pumpkin and sweet potatoes, he and his wife ate it with the greatest relish – the feeling that justice had found its own way of being done.

Cinderella

from First Fairy Tales

Margaret Mayo ✴ Selina Young

Once upon a time, there was a beautiful girl called
Cinderella. She had two ugly stepsisters who were
very unkind and made her do all the hard work. She
had to sweep the floors, cook the food and wash the
dirty dishes, while they dressed up in fine clothes and
went to lots of parties.

One day a special invitation arrived at Cinderella's house. It was from the royal palace. The king's only son, who was a truly handsome prince, was going to have a grand ball, and the three girls were invited to come!

Cinderella knew she wouldn't be allowed to go to the ball. But the ugly sisters... oh! they were excited. They couldn't talk about anything else.

When the day of the ball came, they made such a fuss. Poor Cinderella had to rush about, upstairs and downstairs. She fixed their hair in fancy curls.

She helped them put on their expensive new dresses. And she arranged their jewels, just so!

As soon as they had gone, Cinderella sat down by the fire, and she said, "I do wish I could go to the ball!"

The next moment, standing beside her was a lovely old lady with a silver wand in her hand.

"Cinderella," she said, "I am your fairy godmother, and you *shall* go to the ball! But, first, you must go into the garden and pick a golden pumpkin. Then bring me six mice from the mouse-traps, a whiskery rat from the rat-trap and six lizards. You'll find the lizards behind the watering can."

So Cinderella fetched a golden pumpkin, six grey mice, a whiskery rat and six lizards.

The fairy godmother touched them with her wand... and the pumpkin became a golden coach, the mice became six grey horses, the rat became a coachman with the most enormous moustache and the lizards became six footmen dressed in green and yellow.

Then the fairy godmother touched Cinderella with the wand... and her old dress became a golden dress sparkling with jewels, while on her feet was the prettiest pair of glass slippers ever seen.

"Remember," said the fairy godmother, "you must leave the ball before the clock strikes twelve, because at midnight the magic ends."

"Thank you, kind fairy godmother," said Cinderella. And she climbed into the coach.

When Cinderella arrived at the ball, she looked so beautiful that everyone wondered who she was. Even the ugly sisters! The prince, of course, asked her to dance with him, and they danced all evening. He would not dance with anyone else.

Now Cinderella was enjoying the ball so much that she forgot her fairy godmother's warning, until it was almost midnight and the clock began to strike.

One ... two ... three ... she hurried out of the ballroom. Four ... five ... six ... as she ran down the palace steps, one of her glass slippers fell off. Seven ... eight ... nine ... she ran on towards the golden coach. Ten ... eleven ... TWELVE!

Then ... there was Cinderella in her old dress. A golden pumpkin lay at her feet, and scampering off down the road were six grey mice, a whiskery rat and

six green lizards. So Cinderella
had to walk home, and by the
time the ugly sisters returned,
she was sitting quietly by
the fire.

Now when Cinderella ran
from the palace, the prince
tried to follow her, and he
found the glass slipper.

He said, "I shall marry
the beautiful girl whose foot
fits this slipper – and only her!"

In the morning the prince went
from house to house with the glass
slipper, and every young lady tried
to squeeze her foot into it. But it
didn't fit any of them.

At last the prince came
to Cinderella's house. First
one ugly sister tried to
squash her foot into the
slipper, but her foot was
too wide and fat. Then the
other ugly sister tried, but her
foot was too long and thin.

"Please," said Cinderella,
"let me try."

"The slipper won't fit you!" said the ugly sisters. "You didn't go to the ball!"

But Cinderella slipped her foot into the glass slipper, and it fitted perfectly. The next moment, standing beside her was the fairy godmother. She touched Cinderella with the wand... and there she was in a golden dress sparkling with jewels, and on her feet was the prettiest pair of glass slippers ever seen.

The ugly sisters were so surprised that, for once, they couldn't think of anything to say! But the prince knew what to say – he asked Cinderella to marry him.

And then there was a happy wedding. Everyone who had gone to the ball was invited – even the ugly sisters! There was wonderful food and lots of music and dancing. And the prince, of course, danced every dance with Cinderella. He would not dance with anyone else!

How the Camel Got His Hump

from Animal Stories

Rudyard Kipling　🌴　Wendy Smith

In the beginning of years, when the world was so new-
and-all, and the Animals were just beginning to work for
Man, there was a Camel, and he lived in the middle of a
Howling Desert because he did not want to work; and
besides, he was a Howler himself. So he ate sticks and
thorns and tamarisks and milkweed and prickles, most
'scruciating idle: and when anybody spoke to him he said
"Humph!" Just "Humph!" and no more.

Presently the Horse came to him on
Monday morning, with a saddle on
his back and a bit in his mouth,
and said, "Camel, O Camel, come
out and trot like the rest of us."

"Humph!" said the Camel;
and the Horse went away
and told the Man.

Presently the Dog came to him, with a stick in his mouth, and said, "Camel, O Camel, come and fetch and carry like the rest of us."

"Humph!" said the Camel; and the Dog went away and told the Man.

Presently the Ox came to him, with a yoke on his neck, and said, "Camel, O Camel, come and plough like the rest of us."

"Humph!" said the Camel; and the Ox went away and told the Man.

At the end of the day the Man called the Horse and the Dog and the Ox together, and said, "Three, O Three, I'm very sorry for you (with the world so new-and-all);

but that Humph-thing in the Desert can't work, or he would have been here by now, so I am going to leave him alone, and you must work double-time to make up for it."

That made the three very angry (with the world so new-and-all), and they held a palaver, and an *indaba*, and a *panchayet*, and a pow-wow on the edge of the Desert; and the Camel came chewing milkweed *most* 'scruciating idle, and laughed at them. Then he said "Humph!" and went away again.

Presently there came along the Djinn in charge of All Deserts, rolling in a cloud of dust (Djinns always travel that way because it is Magic), and he stopped to palaver and pow-wow with the Three.

"Djinn of All Deserts," said the Horse, "*is* it right for anyone to be idle, with the world so new-and-all?"

"Certainly not," said the Djinn.

"Well," said the Horse, "there's a thing in the middle of your Howling Desert (and he's a Howler himself) with a long neck and long legs, and he hasn't done a stroke of work since Monday morning. He won't trot."

"Whew!" said the Djinn, whistling, "that's my Camel, for all the gold in Arabia! What does he say about it?"

"He says 'Humph!'" said the Dog, "and he won't fetch and carry."

"Does he say anything else?"

"Only 'Humph': and he won't plough," said the Ox.

"Very good," said the Djinn. "I'll humph him if you will kindly wait a minute."

The Djinn rolled himself up in his dust-cloak, and took a bearing across the desert, and found the Camel most 'scruciatingly idle, looking at his own reflection in a pool of water.

"My long and bubbling friend," said the Djinn, "what's this I hear of you doing no

work, with the world so new-and-all?"

"Humph!" said the Camel.

The Djinn sat down, with his chin in his hand, and began to think a Great Magic, while the Camel looked at his own reflection in the pool of water.

"You've given the Three extra work ever since Monday morning, all on account of your 'scruciating idleness," said the Djinn; and he went on thinking Magics, with his chin in his hand.

"Humph!" said the Camel.

"I shouldn't say that again if I were you," said the Djinn; "you might say it once too often. Bubbles, I want you to work."

And the Camel said "Humph!" again; but no sooner had he said it than he saw his back, that he was so proud of, puffing up and puffing up into a great lolloping humph.

"Do you see that!" said the Djinn. "That's your very own humph that you've brought upon your very own self by not working. Today is Thursday, and you've done no work since Monday, when the work began. Now you are going to work."

"How can I," said the Camel, "with this humph on my back?"

"That's made a-purpose," said the Djinn, "all because you missed those three days. You will be able to work now for three days without eating, because you can live on your humph: and don't ever say I never did anything for you. Come out of the Desert and go to the Three, and behave. Humph yourself!"

And the Camel humphed himself, humph and all, and went away to join the Three. And from that day to this the Camel always wears a humph (we call it "hump" now, not to hurt his feelings); but he has never yet caught up with the three days that he missed at the beginning of the world, and he has never yet learned how to behave.

FROG

from First Poems

Selina Young

A frog once went out walking,
In the pleasant summer air,
He happened into a barber's shop
And skipped into the chair.
The barber said in disbelief:
"Your brains are surely bare.
How can you have a haircut
When you haven't any hair?"

Anon

Little *Angel

Geraldine McCaughrean   Ian Beck

The night was so cold, full
of snowflake stars. It was
Micah's turn to keep
watch over the sheep,
while the other
shepherds slept.

Suddenly the air was full of singing and the sky blizzard-white with angels.

"Don't be afraid!" cried the Archangel. "Wonderful news! A baby is born tonight called Jesus – a king to save the world! He's in a stable, in Bethlehem! Go and see!"

Then upwards soared the angels. Their singing grew softer, and they were gone.

"We must see the baby! Now! Tonight!" the shepherds exclaimed. "Micah, you stay here. Someone must stay with the sheep."

"Oh, but..." Too late. They were already singing their way across the fields into the dark.

Micah was afraid. "What if a wolf comes?" he whispered.

Somewhere a sheep bleated in the dark. Or did it? The cry came again. Micah strained his ears to hear.

"Help! Help!" It was not very far away.

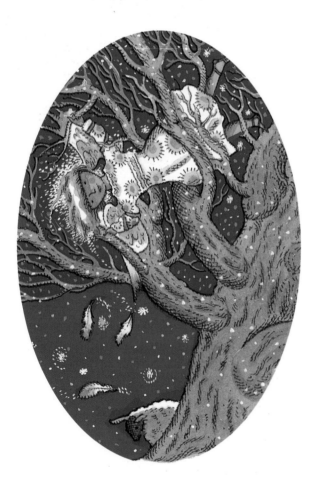

A little angel hung upside down in a tree, her wings in tatters.

"I got caught up," she said. "The others went back to watch over Jesus. I called out for help, but they were singing too loud. They went without me!"

Micah helped her down. "I was left behind too," he said. "Have you seen him? The little king?"

"Oh yes! He was wonderful! Marvellous! I can't describe ... But I must catch them up! In the morning they will leave for the Country of Angels and I may never get home! Only the Archangel can mend my wings."

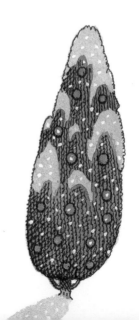
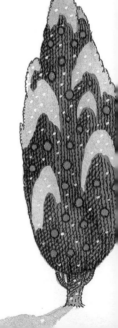

"And I must get back to my flock," said Micah.

"What flock?" asked the little angel.

But for two old ewes, there was not a sheep to be seen.

"A wolf must have come by and scattered them," Micah wailed. "I must find them! I was left in charge!"

"I'll help you look," said the little angel. "Angels are supposed to help people."

"No, no. You must catch up with the other angels," said Micah. "Get your wings mended. Go quickly. I'll manage."

The shepherd boy watched her go. First she stepped into a rabbit hole. Then she tripped over a root. Next she went sprawling into a ditch. Then she sank deep into a bog.

"I think I had better take you there," said Micah, helping her out. "You might meet a wolf on the way."

"It must be wonderful to be a shepherd," said the little angel.

"Oh, but to run messages for God!" said Micah. "To fly in among the planets and stars! That would be fine!"

"For someone who liked high places, I suppose," the little angel said. "But I'm afraid of flying."

The shepherd boy held her hand. "It's wolves with me." He had never told anyone before. "I'm terrified of wolves."

Suddenly a great grey wolf sprang into their path. Its eyes were pale and flecked with red. Its teeth were icicles, dripping.

The shepherd boy felt his heart shrink and his mouth run dry. He stepped in front of the little angel, fumbling for his slingshot.

But all of a sudden, the little angel leapt at the wolf.

Angel and wolf rolled across the ground – grey fur and frayed feathers.

Micah swung his slingshot, but dared not hurl the stone, for fear of hitting his friend.

Then the wolf was on its back ... and the little angel was laughing out loud!

The wolf was grinning and its bushy tail thumped the ground. The little angel was tickling the wolf!

"I like animals," she said.

And they all walked on to Bethlehem.

As they got closer to the town, they thought the streets were full of snow. Then they saw what had become of Micah's sheep.

The sheep had also heard the cry of the angels, and come on a journey of their own to Bethlehem, to the stable.

"I suppose everyone wants to see the newborn king," said Micah.

They could hear the angels singing softly.

"Come in with me," said the little angel.

"Can't," said Micah. "The shepherds would see me. They'd know I left the field."

"They won't see us if we creep in at the back," said the little angel. "And there will never be a more marvellous sight in the history of the world!"

So Micah and the little angel crept inside the stable.

They saw the happy mother and father, saw the donkey and the ox. But best of all, they saw the baby king sleeping peacefully in a box of straw.

Micah opened his eyes wide as wide, so that he would see everything and remember it all, all of his life.

Then they crept outside to where the Archangel was waiting.

"Oh, *there* you are," whispered the Archangel. "I was worried about you. I see you met with a bit of bad luck."

"Not at all," said the little angel, as her drooping wings were mended. "The best luck in the world! I made a friend."

Micah said, "I must drive the sheep back now."

"I'll help you," said the little angel. "Wolf and I." They joined hands for the long walk back. Suddenly Micah's feet rose gently off the ground – "I can fly! I can fly! But how can that be?"

"A touch of the Archangel's wings?" she suggested.

"Or a gift from the baby king," Micah replied.

Below them, Wolf drove the sheep home over the moonlit ground.

"We should change places!" cried the little angel. "I could stay here among the animals, you go flying among the planets!"

"Yes! Because you're not afraid of wolves!" cried Micah "... though of course neither am I any more."

"How strange!" his friend exclaimed. "I'm not afraid of flying either! But how could that be?"

"The touch of the Archangel?" he suggested.

"Or a gift from the baby king," she replied.

Towards morning, the Christmas angels flocked back to the Country of Angels and the littlest angel never again complained at how high they flew.

Each Christmas night after that, while the older shepherds slept and the youngest kept watch, a little angel came visiting from beyond the whirling planets.

Funny Rhymes

from First Poems

Selina Young

Peas

I always eat peas with honey,
I've done it all my life,
They do taste kind of funny
But it keeps them on the knife.

Anon

If All the World...

If all the world were paper,
And all the sea were ink,
And all the trees were bread and cheese,
What should we do for drink?

Anon

An ABC of Names

A is Ann, with milk from the cow.
B is Benjamin, making a row.
C is Charlotte, gathering flowers.
D is Dick, one of the mowers.
E is Eliza, feeding a hen.
F is Frank, mending his pen.
G is Georgiana, shooting an arrow.
H is Harry, wheeling a barrow.
I is Isabella, gathering fruit.
J is John, playing the flute.
K is Kate, nursing her dolly.
L is Lawrence, feeding poor Polly.
M is Maria, learning to draw.

N is Nicholas, with a jackdaw.
O is Octavius, riding a goat.
P is Peter, wearing a coat.
Q is Quintus, armed with a lance.
R is Rachel, learning to dance.
S is Sarah, learning to cook.
T is Tommy, reading a book.
U is Urban, rolling the green.
V is Victoria, reading she's seen.
W is Walter, flying a kite.
X is Xerxes, a boy of great might.
Y is Yvonne, a girl who's been fed.
Z is Zachariah, going to bed.

Anon

STORIES

As children gain in confidence
they soon develop their own
reading tastes and preferences,
discovering the pleasure of
losing themselves in the pages
of a good book.

There's a bountiful
supply of great
stories and poetry

FOR ALL

for them to discover, with fine
new authors emerging all the
time, as well as the classic stories
of previous generations and
other cultures.

Here you will find a selection
of just such stories – so
happy reading!

THE FROG PRINCE

from The Orchard Book of Fairy Tales

Rose Impey   ♥   Ian Beck

In the olden days, when wishing still did some good, there was a king and he had a string of daughters. They were all beautiful, but the youngest was the most beautiful. Even the sun, which had seen some things in its time, blinked whenever it shone into her lovely face.

When the weather was hot and this youngest princess wanted to be cool, she used to wander into a nearby wood and sit in the shade of a tree, by the edge of a deep well. Now, it happened one day that she was sitting there, playing with a golden ball – throwing it up and catching it, throwing it up and catching it, throwing it up and catching it – when it slipped through her fingers, fell into the well and completely disappeared.

This ball was the most treasured thing she had in the world. The girl was so distraught she began to sob as if her heart would break.

Suddenly, up popped a great ugly frog.

"What's wrong, my beauty?" asked the frog. "That crying's enough to melt a heart of stone."

"I've lost my ball. It's fallen into the well and it's so deep I can't even see the bottom. I'll never get it back."

"I can get it back," said the frog. "It's easy."

The princess stopped crying.

Then the frog said, "But what will you give me if I do?"

"My clothes, my pearls and jewels, even this golden crown on my head, anything."

"Anything?" asked the frog.

"Anything in the world," said the princess.

"Jewels and golden crowns are no use to me," said the frog. "But if you promise to be my wife..."

"Your wife!" The princess nearly burst out laughing.

"If you let me live with you and eat off your little golden plate and drink from your little golden cup and sleep in your own little bed... then I'll get it back for you."

The princess thought he must be joking. Marry a frog! It was too silly. Anyway, how could a frog live away from its well? But then she thought, 'Why not humour him?' She would promise him anything, if he would only get her ball.

"Yes, yes," she said, "whatever you like."

The frog closed his big goggle eyes and dived deep into the well. And, in less time than it takes to tell, he reappeared with the ball in his wide-open mouth. But when he threw the ball down, the princess snatched it up and ran off home with it.

"Wait, wait," called the frog. "I can't run as fast as you."

And that was exactly what the princess was relying on. She was soon safe at home and never gave the frog another thought.

But, as you well know, we can't wriggle out of our promises that easily; and neither could she.

The next evening, as the princess sat down for dinner with her family, she heard a flip, flap, flop, coming up the steep marble staircase, then a gentle tapping low down at the door.

There came a croaking noise, which the princess recognised, and it said, "Open the door, youngest born."

The princess ran to the door and opened it. But when she saw the frog sitting there, she slammed the door shut and hurried back to her place at the table. She sat there shaking, as if she'd seen her own ghost.

"My dear," said the king. "Who was it? You look as if an ogre had come to carry you away."

"Almost as bad, Father," said she. "It's a great ugly frog that I met yesterday. I lost my golden ball in the well and, because I was so upset, he got it back for me. But, in return, he made me promise to marry him and let him live with me."

Just then the voice came again:

"Open the door, my love, my life.
Open the door, sweet lady.
Remember you swore to be my wife.
That was the promise you made me."

"Well," said the king. "A promise is a promise and must be kept. Let the frog in."

The princess went and opened the door and in hopped the frog, flip, flop, flip, flop, across the table. Then it said,

"Lift me up, my love, my life.
Lift me up, sweet lady.
I want to sit in the lap of my wife.
Remember the promise you made me."

But the princess couldn't even bring herself to touch the clammy frog and she went on sitting there, ignoring him, until the king insisted.

"A promise is a promise and must be kept."

So she took the frog up on her knee. But next he wanted to be on the table, and then, when he was on the table, he still wasn't satisfied.

"Move your plate closer, my love, my life.
Share your food with me, sweet lady.
Such is the act of a loving wife.
Remember the promise you made me."

The princess knew she would have to do it, yet she hated every moment. She sat there, hardly able to look at him. The frog ate a hearty meal, but the food stuck in the princess's throat, so that she felt she would be sick.

When the great ugly frog had eaten until he was quite bloated with food, he said:

"Take me to bed, my love, my life.
Take me to bed, sweet lady.
From now on you are my wife.
Remember the promise you made me."

At this the princess began to cry. The thought of that cold, wet creature in her own little bed was too much to bear. She couldn't do it; she wouldn't do it; no one could make her. But the king could. He was angry.

"This is no way to treat someone who helps you when you most need it. Don't look down on him now."

So the princess picked up the frog between two fingers and held him at a distance. This way she carried him all the way up the stairs until they were alone in her bedroom. Then she placed the frog in the corner, farthest from her bed, and hoped he would stay there.

But later, when she was lying in the dark, the frog crept over, flip, flop, flip, flop, and said, "Princess, lift me up and let me sleep with you in your little bed. I'll be more comfortable there." The princess hesitated, but the frog added, "Or I'll tell your father."

And the princess knew only too well what the king would say. So she lifted the frog up and placed him beside her on the pillow. Then she squeezed herself on to the very edge of the bed, as far as she could from the clammy creature.

But now, horror of horrors, what do you think he said next?

"Come much closer, my love, my life.
Come much closer, sweet lady.
Kiss my lips, my own dear wife.
Remember the promise you made me."

At this the princess was in an agony of disgust. But she closed her eyes and turned her face to the detested animal. Determined to get it over as quickly as she could, she pursed up her lips ready and leaned forward.

For a moment she allowed herself to imagine the feel of his cold, wet skin against her own. It made her shiver. But when her lips touched his she was amazed to feel instead that they were soft and warm, certainly not frog-like.

The princess opened her eyes. She expected to be looking into the great goggle eyes of the frog, but she wasn't. She was looking into the dark, smiling eyes of a handsome prince. Oh, the relief!

Then he told her such a story, of how he had been enchanted by a wicked fairy and destined to stay that way until a princess rescued him. And she'd been the one to do it.

Well, with her so beautiful and him so handsome, you'll soon guess the outcome. He asked her to marry him and return with him to his father's kingdom. And the next day there arrived the most elegant coach with eight plumed horses to pull it, which carried them home. There they lived happily for the rest of their lives. And if they lived happily, well then, why shouldn't we also?

The Emperor's New Clothes

from Stories from Hans Andersen

Andrew Matthews Alan Snow

The emperor was mad about clothes. He changed his coat every time the palace clock struck the hour, his shoes every half hour and his hat every ten minutes. In fact, the emperor had no time for anything else.

"Fashions keep changing," he informed his prime minister, "and I must change to keep up with them."

One day, two strangers arrived at the palace. They said they were weavers with important news for the emperor, but they were really a pair of swindlers. When they met the emperor, they nudged one another and sniggered.

"Is something funny?" the emperor asked sternly.

"We couldn't help laughing at your clothes," the swindlers replied.

"What's wrong with my clothes?" the emperor asked anxiously.

"Out of date!" declared the swindlers. "No one wears silk shirts nowadays! And your coat might have been in fashion once, but not any more. It's lucky for you that we came along. We can weave a cloth so beautiful it will never go out of fashion. Once you're wearing a suit made from our special cloth, you'll be the envy of every fashionable person in the world!"

These words put an excited gleam in the emperor's eyes.

"Really?" he murmured.

"There are a couple of problems, though," one of the swindlers said slyly. "The cloth is very expensive for one thing, and for another – it can't be seen by people who are stupid or who aren't doing their work properly."

"Amazing!" the emperor whispered to himself. "Not only will I be the best-dressed person on earth, but I'll be able to tell which ministers are wise and which are foolish!" He smiled at the swindlers. "Weave me

enough cloth for a new suit at once! Take as much gold from the treasury as you need."

The swindlers set up a loom in the corner of the palace and pretended to be hard at work, even though the loom was half-empty – unlike their pockets, which jingled with gold coins.

After a day or two, the emperor spoke to the prime minister.

"I want to know how the special cloth is coming on. You're a wise sort of chap, go and see for yourself, then report back to me."

The prime minister did as the emperor asked, but when he entered the room where the swindlers were working and saw the empty loom, he turned pale.

"I can't see a thing!" he said to himself. "I must be stupid! If the emperor finds out, I'll lose my job!"

"Well, prime minister?" smiled the swindlers. "What do you think of it?"

"Er… wonderful!" gulped the prime minister. "Such an unusual shade! Such a marvellous pattern! I can't wait to tell the emperor about it."

It didn't take long for news of the wonderful cloth to spread. The emperor had so many requests to view the material that when he finally saw it for himself he was surrounded by a group of very important people.

When the swindlers entered, carrying nothing, and spread nothing out like a big roll of cloth, there was complete silence. No one could see anything. Everyone waited for someone else to speak first because they were afraid of being thought foolish.

"Oh, magnificent!" cooed the prime minister at last. "That purple edge brings the pattern out perfectly!"

"But I can't see anything!" thought the emperor. "What if someone finds out that I am a stupid emperor who can't do his job properly?" Out loud, he said, "Marvellous!"

And at once, all the important people chattered about how beautiful the cloth looked, while the swindlers shook with silent giggles.

"In three days it will be my birthday parade," the emperor told the rogues. "I want you to make me a suit that my subjects will marvel at!"

The two rogues spent hours snipping at thin air with golden scissors and sewing nothing together with silver needles. On the morning of the emperor's birthday, they sent him a message saying that the new clothes were ready.

The emperor arrived with two servants. The swindlers smiled broadly and held out their empty hands.

"Here are the trousers and coat, Your Majesty," said one.

"And here is your long cloak," said the other. "If Your Majesty would

take off all your clothes and stand in front of that big mirror, we shall help you dress."

The emperor did just as the weavers said and let them move around him, making him step into the imaginary trousers and pull on the imaginary coat.

"I can hardly feel the cloth against my skin, it's so fine," said the emperor. He turned to his servants. "Hold up the edge of the cloak so that it doesn't drag on the ground," he said.

The two servants looked at the floor and frowned deeply.

"What's the matter?" asked the emperor. "Are you both too foolish to see it?"

"I've got it, Your Majesty!" cried one servant, bending down.

"So have I!" exclaimed the other.

And they both stood as though they were holding the cloak in their hands.

The swindlers left the palace faster than dragonflies, while the emperor went off on his parade. The streets were packed with people, all pretending that they were wise and could see the emperor's clothes.

"Hurrah for the emperor!" they shouted. "Hurrah for his new suit!"

And everybody cheered – except one little boy. He didn't know anything about the emperor's clothes. He had been too busy playing to hear the story, and grown-ups talked about such boring things that he never listened to them anyway. When he saw the emperor waddling along, he blushed deep red.

"There's a man with no clothes on!" he gasped.

"Hush!" said his father. "That's the emperor."

"But why hasn't he got any clothes on?" shouted the little boy.

At the sound of his shout, the cheering stopped. Whispers began to run through the crowd.

"The boy's right!"

"The emperor isn't wearing anything!"

"The emperor's got no clothes on at all!"

The whispers reached the ears of the emperor, and he began to worry that they might be true.

"It can't be helped now," he told himself. "The parade must go on."

And he marched ahead more proudly than ever, followed at a distance by his ministers and the two servants, who went on holding the cloak that wasn't there.

And that's the end of the story.

ALL ABOUT MY FAMILY

from Peculiar Rhymes and Lunatic Lines

Max Fatchen • Lesley Bisseker

What sends our family into shock
Is the frantic search for a missing sock.

What makes our family fly into rages
Is people who stay in the bathroom for ages.

BROTHER BOTHER

My brother doesn't wash his face,
His hair is never trim.
My brother's not afraid of germs
But they're afraid of him.

I showed my brother the shining stars.
I thought it was a favour.
I pointed out the Milky Way,
He stared and said: "What flavour?"

(big mouth).

SISTER SOUNDS

I can't understand it,
Can you?
But it's true
That whales are enormous.
Yet they speak
With a tiny squeal
And a gentle squeak.
But my sister,
Who's only two,
Makes the most awful
Hullaballoo.

I can't understand it,
Can you?

WATCH IT

A mother is wise,
So people have said,
And seems to have eyes in the
Back of her head.
But I'll be honest,
And I'll be blunt,
My mother sees plenty
From hers in front.

MISSED AGAIN

My father's not terribly smart
At hitting a board with a dart.
It's rather a shame
That when he takes aim,
People lie on the floor or depart.

The Wooden Horse

from The Orchard Book of Greek Myths

Geraldine McCaughrean   ❖   Emma Chichester Clark

There was once a woman who was hatched from an egg, like a bird. But she was more beautiful than any bird that ever flew. She was called Helen and there was not a prince, nor a duke, nor a king who did not want to win her. But she married old King Menelaus and lived in a palace on the shores of his kingdom.

If only that had put an end to the hopes of all the other princes, dukes and kings! Young, handsome Paris, Prince of Troy, found Helen too beautiful to forget, and wanted too much to have her for his own. So he stole Helen's love and ran away with her to Troy – the city called the City of Horses.

King Menelaus grieved – but his grief then turned to anger – and, calling together an army of fifty thousand men, he sailed for Troy to get back his wife. He took with him the greatest heroes of the world: Achilles the brave, Odysseus the cunning, and Ajax the proud. A thousand ships put ashore outside the tall white walls of Troy.

Helen looked out of her palace window and saw the fleet approaching.

"What will happen now?" she wondered. "Who will win me? Which side do I *want* to win?"

For weeks, for months, for years the Greeks lay siege to the city. The great heroes of Troy fought in single combat with the great heroes of

Greece, sword against sword, chariot against chariot. But it decided nothing. After ten years, Achilles the brave was dead. Ajax the proud lay in a grave covered with flowers. And Paris too was dead and his lips too cold for kissing. So many good men had been killed. And those who had lived were sadder, wearier, older. Only Helen remained as lovely as ever – a precious prize locked inside Troy.

At last Odysseus the cunning spoke up. "I think I know how we can get inside the city of Troy." The Greeks listened eagerly.

"It'll never work!" said some.

"It's too dangerous!" said others.

But the old King Menelaus nodded and said, "Do it, Odysseus."

For days the Trojans, inside their walls, could hear nothing but sawing and hammering.

Then one morning they looked over their high walls and saw ... a horse. A huge wooden horse.

They also saw that the Greeks had packed up their tents, launched their ships and set sail. "They've gone! They've gone!" cheered the Trojans. "We've won the war! ... But what's this they've left behind? A horse?" They crept outside to look.

"It's a tribute to Troy!" said some. "A tribute to the City of Horses!"

"It's a trick," said others.

One old man threw a spear at the wooden horse and it struck with a hollow thud. "Beware of Greeks even when they give you presents!" he warned.

But the people of Troy would not listen. "Don't be so dismal! The war's over! The Greeks have gone, haven't they?"

They began to celebrate, to drink wine and to dance. And they towed the huge wooden horse, on long ropes, in through the gates of Troy.

Meanwhile, inside the horse's hollow body, a dozen Greek soldiers crouched as still as stones. There was so little room in their hiding place that they were all pressed together, knee against knee, elbow against ear.

"Heave!" cried the Trojans, as they pulled the giant horse into the city square. The bumpy ride jogged and bruised the men hidden inside, but they held their breath and gripped their swords tight. One sneeze and they would be found out!

Helen looked out of her window and saw the horse, all decorated now with flowers and ribbons. She was a Greek and knew the ways of the Greeks and she thought to herself, "This is a trick." She turned away from the window, put a finger to her lips and sat quite still, waiting.

The happy Trojans danced all day round the long legs of the wooden horse. At last, weary with joy, they tottered home to sleep, and the city fell silent.

Then a secret door creaked open in the stomach of the horse. Down dropped a knotted rope. Down the rope climbed the dozen Greeks.

Meanwhile, the whole Greek fleet of ships sailed back to shore: they had only been hiding over the sea's horizon, waiting. As they pelted up the beach, they peered through the early morning darkness at the high, heavy city gates, anxious to see whether their plan had succeeded.

And there! The gates creaked open to let them in and the Greeks dashed through, swords at the ready. A war that had lasted ten years was over. They set light to Troy's tall buildings. They killed Troy's young men. Then they seized Helen and sailed away. By morning there was nothing but the sound of weeping within Troy's charred and crumbling walls.

And Helen lived once more in the palace of King Menelaus on the shores of his kingdom. If she had loved Paris once, she never said so, and never spoke his name, and she and Menelaus lived happily ever after.

BILLY BEAST

A Seriously Silly Story

Laurence Anholt ✳ Arthur Robins

Betty and Benjamin Beast were very proud of their castle. They thought it was the most wonderful building for miles around.

It had taken them years to get it just right with lovely green mouldy walls and black puddles in the corridors. There were damp, dark

bedrooms with snails on the pillows, and smelly cellars too.

At weekends, you would always find Benjamin up a stepladder whistling happily as he hung new cobwebs in corners or painted fresh mud on the ceilings. And when their beastly friends came for dinner, it was hard not to show off the new kitchen with its sweet little scampering cockroaches in all the cupboards, and hot and cold running slime in the taps.

There was only one thing that Betty and Benjamin were more proud of than their home, and that was their fine young son, Billy Beast. They loved Billy more than words can say.

The truth is, Billy was a bit spoiled. They were always giving him some little treat or other – an enormous pet toad in a box, or as much crunchy earwig ice-cream as a beastly boy could eat, which wasn't very good for him. Billy always had the best of everything – even private belching lessons after Beastie School.

By the time he was sixteen Billy had grown into a fine-looking beast. He was tall and strong with plenty of fleas in his hair and the sharpest brown teeth a beast could

wish for. There wasn't a girl beast around who wasn't in love with young Billy, with those twinkling yellow eyes and that cute way he had of wiping his snout with the hairs on the back of his hand – who could resist him? But as far as Benjamin and Betty were concerned, it would have to be a very special girl beast who could be disgusting enough to marry their son.

So the three of them just carried on living happily together from day to day. Billy and his toad practised their burping and everyone who met the Beast family thought they were the luckiest, smelliest, most horribly beautiful family they had ever met.

Then one morning, Benjamin and Betty went out gathering frog spawn for lunch, leaving young Billy playing quietly with his toad in his bedroom. Billy heard a noise outside, and when he looked out of the window he saw an old man wandering about in their beautiful weedy garden.

The man had tied his horse to the tree and he was busy *stealing* some of Betty's prize-winning roses!

"Hoi! What do you think you're doing?" shouted Billy. "This is a private castle, you know. My mum will eat you if she catches you here."

When the man looked up at the castle and saw young Billy Beast all hairy and horrid with a big toad sitting on his head he was *absolutely terrified*!

"Oh p-please don't eat me, Mr Beast," he stammered. "I got lost and... and I promised my beautiful daughter I would bring her a red rose and..."

"Well, not from our garden, pal!" snorted Billy.

The man was so frightened, that

he promised that he would send his daughter, Beauty, to marry Billy if he was allowed to go free.

"All right," Billy agreed, "but she'd better come soon or my dad will be after you too."

"I...I'll send her straight away," said the poor man, jumping on to his horse.

"And she'd better be as beautiful as you say," Billy called after him.

"Oh yes, oh yes, she is!" shouted the man, riding away as fast as he could. "There's nothing in the world more beautiful than my daughter."

"What? More beautiful than my toad?" called Billy.

But the man was already out of sight.

When Betty and Benjamin came home, Billy told them the whole story.

"I'm going to be married," he grunted happily, "to the most beautiful girl in the world – the man said there's nothing in the world more beautiful than Beauty."

Betty and Benjamin were very pleased to think of their son married to the most beautiful girl in the world, although they found it hard to believe that anyone could be quite as good-looking as their Billy.

Early next morning, Beauty arrived. Billy saw her horse coming up the hill towards the castle. He quickly ran to the mirror to make sure his teeth were nice and black and he checked that his breath was good and smelly.

303

He splashed a little skunk juice under his arms, then he ran to the door to meet his bride.

Billy was very excited. As the doorbell rang, he twisted his face into the most beautifully disgusting shape that he could manage, then pulled open the door.

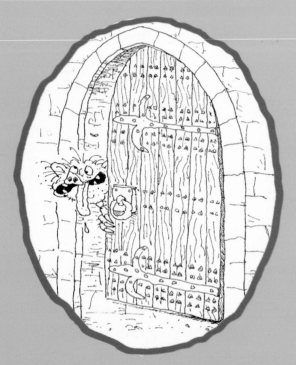

She was hardly hairy at all, except on her head. And her *teeth* – they were all sort of white and shiny! She had a horrid pink *nose* where her snout should be, and little *fingers* instead of nice claws! UGH! It was *disgusting*!

"I bet she hasn't even got a hairy chest," thought Billy in dismay.

When Beauty saw Billy, she almost fainted on the spot. Billy could understand that, because his handsome looks often made girls feel weak at the knees. What he couldn't understand was that Beauty wasn't beautiful! In fact she looked just like an ordinary *girl*!

Betty and Benjamin were also disappointed, but they tried not to show it. The poor girl had come a long way to marry their son and she seemed upset too.

"I'm sure she will look better once we get rid of that nasty white dress and pop her into a nice sloppy mud bath," said Betty kindly.

"And she'll probably get hairier as she gets older," suggested Benjamin. "Perhaps she hasn't been eating a healthy diet – I expect she's hungry now after that long journey. Let's start her off with a lovely bowl of warm earwax and slug juice."

So Betty and Benjamin set about

trying to make Beauty a little more beastly, and Billy went into the garden with his toad and sulked.

After a few days, Beauty began to get used to living with the Beasts, and Billy had to admit that she was looking a little better; at least she was getting more smelly.

But then Beauty would go and spoil it all by doing something revolting like washing her hands before a meal, or combing her hair and everyone realised that no matter how they tried, Beauty would never be truly disgusting.

Billy promised his parents that he would try to get along with her, although he swore he would never marry her. He patiently taught her to burp nicely and to dribble, but she was slow to learn.

Then one morning in the garden, something horrid happened. Billy had just allowed Beauty to play with his toad when she turned around and tried to *kiss him!* He wiped his mouth and jumped away.

what you look like, it's the person inside that counts.

Before he knew what he was doing, Billy had put down his toad and taken Beauty into his hairy arms, he put his snout close to her little head and ... SMACK! He kissed her tiny snubby nose.

Beauty began to cry. "I can't help it!" she wailed, "I can't help looking like this. Of course I would like to be hairy and horrid like you. But couldn't you try to love me for what I am instead of the way I look?"

Now Billy was really a kind-hearted beast. He began to feel sorry for Beauty. He saw that she was right. It doesn't really matter

Right before Billy's yellow eyes, Beauty began to change! She grew hairier

and hairier. Her teeth grew brown and longer. Her fingers turned into beautiful claws!

At last she stood before him – a truly wonderful beastie girl, with the most

gorgeous damp snout Billy had ever seen, and a delightful smell of old socks and kangaroo sweat.

Beauty explained that the man who had stolen the roses was not her father, but a wicked wizard who had cast a spell on her. She would lose her beastly looks until the day someone like Billy was kind enough to kiss her and break the spell.

Billy was so happy, he didn't know what to say, so he just dribbled a little. The beastly couple skipped happily up the steps of the castle, claw in claw, burping excitedly to each other.

And they were all disgustingly happy for the rest of their beastly lives.

THE LOBSTER QUADRILLE

from Down in the Marvellous Deep
Sophie Windham

"Will you walk a little faster?" said a whiting to a snail.
"There's a porpoise close behind us, and he's treading on
    my tail.
See how eagerly the lobsters and the turtles all advance!
They are waiting on the shingle – will you come and join
    the dance?
    Will you, won't you, will you, won't you, will you join
      the dance?
    Will you, won't you, will you, won't you, won't you
      join the dance?"

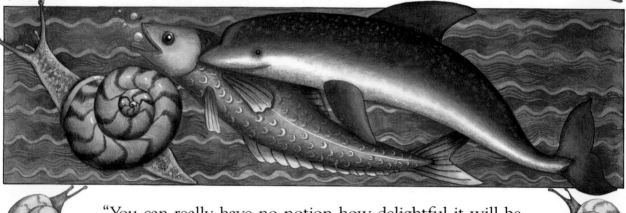

"You can really have no notion how delightful it will be,
When they take us up and throw us, with the lobsters, out
    to sea!"
But the snail replied, "Too far, too far!" and gave a look
    askance –
Said he thanked the whiting kindly, but he would not join
    the dance.
    Would not, could not, would not, could not, would not
      join the dance.
    Would not, could not, would not, could not, could not
      join the dance.

"What matters it how far we go?" his scaly friend replied,
"There is another shore, you know, upon the other side.
The further off from England the nearer is to France –
Then turn not pale, beloved snail, but come and join the
        dance.
    Will you, won't you, will you, won't you, will you join
        the dance?
    Will you, won't you, will you, won't you, won't you
    join the dance?"

                                                    Lewis Carroll

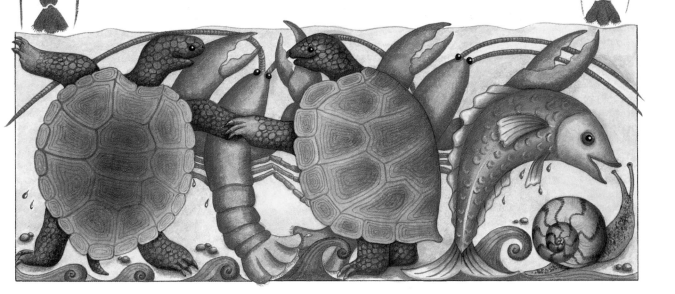

THE CHILDREN OF LIR

from The Orchard Book of Irish Fairy Tales and Legends

Una Leavy   ❖   Susan Field

There was once a race of people in Ireland called the Tuatha Dé Danann. They knew about magic and casting spells. One of them, Lir, was a king. He lived happily with his wife and four children.

One dreadful day his wife became ill and died. Lir and the children were heartbroken.

"Don't worry, Father," his daughter, Finnuala, said some time later. "I will look after my little brothers."

"You are too young," said Lir gently. "Children need a mother. Some day I will marry again."

One day in summer, Lir had a visitor. It was Aoife, his wife's sister. She hugged the children and smiled at Lir. Her eyes were dark as elderberries, her skin creamy as milk.

"It's such a sunny day," she said. "Let's eat outside. You must not be sad any more."

The children were delighted and Lir fell in love with her at once. Aoife would make a perfect wife and mother ...

Aoife too was pleased.

'My plan is working,' she thought. 'Soon I will be queen. Lir is rich and will give me anything I ask for. But those children are a nuisance. When we are married, I will get rid of them.'

A sudden wind howled round the fort and clouds buried the sun ...

Soon there was a royal wedding. It lasted for days, then Lir and his bride travelled the kingdom.

"How beautiful his wife is!" people said.

But one old man shook his head.

"Haven't you noticed?" he asked. "Wherever she walks, the wind howls, and clouds bury the sun. This woman will bring trouble."

But they only laughed at him.

"Don't be silly! It's just the weather!" they said.

At last Lir and his new wife returned home. Aoife went inside to try on her new jewels and robes. Lir walked contentedly outside his fort. His four children were playing on the lawn.

'How good they are,' he thought to himself, 'and how quickly they are growing! I must spend more time with them.'

So every day after that he played with the children – and spent a little less time with his wife.

Aoife noticed. She began to get restless. She did not enjoy swimming or fishing with the children. She felt bored and left out. Lir was rich – he could go anywhere, get anything he wanted. Why did she have to stay at home while he rambled off on stupid adventures with those children? Lir loved them, that was why, maybe more than he loved Aoife.

As time went on, Aoife grew more and more jealous.

'Only for the children,' she thought, 'I would have Lir all to myself. I must get rid of them.'

One day, she spoke sweetly to her husband.

"My dear," she said, "the children are growing up now and don't need us. It will be good for them to go away from home. We can have such wonderful times together, just the two of us."

"No, Aoife," Lir replied. "Those children are part of me. I would die without them."

Time after time she tried to persuade him, but it was no use.

Aoife became desperate. A terrible idea took hold in her head. It choked her heart and smothered her brain, until one day she thought of a dreadful plan...

It was summer. All was still in the drowsy heat. Lir dozed in a shady corner as Aoife called to him.

"I am taking the children to swim in the lake. It is so warm."

Lir was pleased. He had begun to think lately that Aoife was not

completely happy. She hadn't played with the children for such a long time. Lazily waving goodbye, he settled down for a snooze...

The children enjoyed the chariot ride. Soon they were tumbling down the hill and into the lake. Laughing and splashing, they chased each other in the cool fresh water. Heat shimmered in the bushes across the lake. Everything was still – it was too hot even for the birds.

Suddenly Aoife, lifting up her arms, began to chant strange words. The sun darkened, a chill wind whipped over the waves. Finnuala watched uneasily. She turned to her brothers, but they were staring at her in horror.

"Finnuala! Your hair! What's happening to your hair?"

Finnuala looked down. Her long dark hair no longer swirled around her in the water. Even as she looked, white feathers grew over her shoulders covering her skin, and in place of her arms were two wings!

Too frightened to scream, Finnuala looked
back at her brothers. She was just in time
to see their rosy cheeks disappear as
they too were covered in smooth white
feathers. Finnuala and her brothers had
been changed into swans!

There was a mighty clap of thunder.
Spears of rain lashed around her,
but Aoife didn't care. Her spell
had succeeded – now she had
nothing to fear!

Then one of the swans began to
speak, for Aoife's magic had failed
to destroy their voices.

"What have you done to us?"
Finnuala cried. "Why have you done
this wicked deed?"

Aoife laughed.

"Lir is mine now, all mine!" she
screeched. "And you – you will remain as
swans for nine hundred years! You will spend the first three hundred on
this lake, three hundred in the Sea of Moyle and the last three hundred
on Inish Glora in the west. You will never be human again until you
hear the sound of a holy man's bell! Now get away from here! I will
never have to look at you again!"

And though the swans called to her and begged her to have pity
on them, she would not listen. She climbed up the hill by Lough
Derravarragh and hurried away.

The sun shone again, the water lapped gently on the shore, but Finnuala and her brothers could only huddle together. They tried to comfort each other.

"Our father will save us," Finnuala said. "You know how much he loves us. He has all the powers of the Tuatha Dé Danann. Don't cry, little brothers, we will soon be home again."

When she reached the fort, Aoife tiptoed over to the sleeping Lir and gently kissed him.

"Wake up, Lir dear," she said. "I have sad news. Your four children drowned in the lake. But don't fret – I will take care of you. Now we are alone at last..."

"Drowned! How? What... what happened? Oh, my children! My children!"

And flinging Aoife aside, Lir ran like a madman towards the lake, yelling their names, gasping and sobbing. But when he reached it, there was nothing to be seen except the softly lapping water ... and four swans.

Lir threw himself to the ground, rocking back and forth in sorrow and despair. Then a voice spoke to him.

"Father, don't grieve. We are not

dead. Aoife has changed us into swans. It is Finnuala who speaks."

Lifting his head, Lir almost forgot to breathe as the biggest swan told him of his wife's evil deed.

"Oh, my children!" he cried. "My poor beautiful children! But don't despair. I will make Aoife take back this wicked spell. Stay here – I will soon be back."

And he rushed off to the fort.

Aoife sat calmly brushing her hair.

"What have you done?" cried Lir, shaking her by the shoulders. "Are you crazy? You know how much I love those children. How could you do such a thing? Come at once and take back that wicked spell!"

"No, Lir," Aoife replied. "You are all mine now. Your children have gone – who cares about a few swans?"

Lir begged and pleaded and threatened and screamed, but Aoife went on brushing her beautiful hair.

Then Lir called on the powers of his god-ancestors and in a terrifying rage he changed Aoife into a demon. With a terrible screech, she vanished into the air, leaving only a trickle of ashes and the stench of burning hair...

Lir rushed back to the shore and told the children all that had happened. And though he tried and tried, he could not free them from Aoife's awful spell. He cried as he touched them, stroking their feathers. Now there was no power on earth that could save them.

All that long day, Lir stayed on the shore and when night came he would not go home. "You will get cold," his servants said. "And it looks like rain. Tomorrow you can come again."

But he would not leave. So they built a little fire to keep him warm. Friends came to keep him company, for the news had spread. When morning came, more and more people arrived to comfort Lir – and some just to stare...

Eventually Lir had a hut built on the shore. He slept here at night and spent every day with the swans. He mourned for his children, but at least he could speak with them.

Years passed. Lir grew old. One wet winter day he caught cold. His poor tired heart could not take any more and he died. The swans were heartbroken. In time, the hut rotted away and people stopped coming to the lake.

Winters came and went. All the time, Finnuala cared for her brothers and tried to keep them cheerful and brave.

At last, three hundred years were over. The people who had known Lir and his children were long since dead. One morning, the swans left the lake and flew north to the Sea of Moyle. Only one little girl, looking upwards, wondered if they were the children of Lir...

The Sea of Moyle was harsh and wild. North winds lashed with icy splinters, snow whirled so fast that the swans could scarcely see. Time after time, they were dashed apart, their feathers stiff with ice. Winter gales hurtled them towards sharpened rocks. But, whenever she could, Finnuala kept her brothers under her wings, singing to them the songs they knew when they were children. She reminded them of happy times that were past and the wonderful days they had spent with their father. And somehow they survived those three hundred long, bitter years.

When their time was up, the swans gladly flew south-west. They landed on the island of Inish Glora. The wild Atlantic was rough and cold, but nothing could be worse than what they had already endured.

Here, summer brought gentle winds and sunshine to warm their bones. By now the swans were tired and old. They had almost forgotten how to speak. Still Finnuala encouraged them and reminded them of Aoife's words – that, one day, they would be set free by the sound of a holy man's bell ...

And so the time went on. One evening as the sun set, Finnuala lifted her head, listening. Yes, there it was again – the clear, sweet ringing of a bell.

"Surely this is the sound we have been waiting for!" she cried. "Let's go ashore at once!"

They stumbled on to the strand. Clumsily they climbed up a steep grassy path to a group of stone huts. A man came out. He was surprised to see swans at his door, but when Finnuala spoke he staggered back.

"Don't go!" she begged. "My brothers and I need you. Please, listen!"

She told him their story and all that Aoife had said.

"You are safe now," said the man when he heard. "That was the sound of holy Patrick's bell. I will take care of you for the rest of your days."

The good man kept his word. He fed the swans and made them a cosy nest. Night after night he listened as they told him of times long gone and all that had happened since. Then, one day, as he reached out to touch them, their feathers fell away. Finnuala and her brothers were human again. They were nine hundred years old. The good man had scarcely blessed them when they died. Tenderly he buried them in one grave.

That night five stars swooped across the glittering sky. He knew then that Lir and his children were together again, in some beautiful, far-off place...

An extract from

KING ARTHUR

Andrew Matthews 👑 Peter Utton

ar raged for sixteen years. Villages were burned down. Men were too busy fighting to harvest and ungathered crops rotted in the fields. The air was thick with smoke and the wailing of new widows and orphans. The whole country was caught up in the fighting and the misery, hunger and disease that civil war brings with it.

At last, the great lords called a truce. They said that they were sick of war. Just before Christmas they met together in the hall of the cathedral at London to see if they could settle their arguments. First there was feasting and laughter, then there were curses and insults, and suddenly swords were drawn.

"Stop this!" thundered a voice.

The voice was loud enough for everyone to hear and cold enough to freeze them where they stood. Merlin walked through the hall, staring straight into the eyes of each man as he passed. No one could hold the Enchanter's gaze for long.

"While you squabble like dogs over a bone, Britain lies in ruins!" Merlin scolded. "It's time for peace!"

"There'll be no peace until we have a king!" said one of the lords. "Choose one of us, Merlin!"

Other voices called out in agreement, but Merlin shook his head. "High kings are born, not chosen," he said. "But I will make you a magic that will find him." Merlin circled his hands in the air and a light shone in through the windows of the hall. The light was so bright that the men covered their eyes.

"Follow me," said Merlin. "See what I have done."

It was cold outside the hall and the twilight air was grey. There in the churchyard stood a block of pure white marble. On top of the marble was an iron anvil and sunk deep into the anvil was a sword. The jewels on the hilt of the sword glowed softly in the last of the daylight. Written on the block in letters of gold were the words:

'Whoever draws this sword from the anvil and the stone is the true-born High King of Britain.'

"Go back to your castles," commanded Merlin. "Send messengers out to every knight in the land. Tell them that a tournament will be held in London on New Year's Day. The champions of the tournament will be the first to try and draw the sword."

The crowd of noblemen slowly left the churchyard until at last only one knight remained. It was Sir Gawain, a young man who was famous for his courage and his skills in battle. He gazed at the sword in the anvil and was deep in thought.

"What is it, Gawain?" Merlin asked. "Do you want to try and draw the sword?"

"Not me!" laughed Gawain. "I'm no true-born high king. But I'll fight on the side of the man who is, even if he turns out to be my worst enemy!"

"He won't be," Merlin said. "You and the high king will be close friends."

"You know who he is already, don't you?" said Gawain. Merlin said nothing, but he smiled. It was a thin, strange smile.

rthur was a squire. That meant he could wear a short sword at his belt and dress in fine clothes on special occasions, but it also meant he was at the beck and call of his older brother, Kay. Kay was already a knight and should have known better, but he seemed to enjoy ordering Arthur about. He even made Arthur empty out his bathwater and groom his horse, treating him more like a servant than a squire and a brother.

Arthur could have complained to their father, but he knew that Sir Ector would only take Kay's part. Kay was the favourite and Sir Ector made no secret of it. Besides, Arthur wanted Kay to like him and he thought the best way to go about it was to do everything that Kay wanted without grumbling.

When he wasn't being Kay's skivvy, Arthur learned about being a knight. As a small boy, he had imagined that being taught how to hold a lance and use a sword would be exciting – but it wasn't. It was mostly doing the same things over and over again and still getting them wrong. His trainer, the master-at-arms, was stern but fair.

"You've got a lot to learn, but there's the makings of a knight in you, lad," he kept telling Arthur.

Arthur hated being called a lad. He was nearly as tall as Kay and felt quite grown up, but everyone treated him as though he was still a child.

The Christmas after Arthur's sixteenth birthday, a mysterious messenger arrived at the castle. Sir Ector saw him in private and then sent a servant to fetch Kay.

"Can't I go as well?" Arthur asked his brother.

"This is knights' business, not squires'," Kay replied haughtily. "Why don't you run along and play, like a good little boy?"

Arthur was dying to give Kay a kick for this insult, but he knew it would only cause trouble, so he went out into the courtyard to find a stone to kick instead. He noticed the messenger's servant guarding his master's horse. Arthur strolled over and pretended to admire the animal. Before long, he and the servant started to chat.

"There's going to be a big tournament in London," the servant said. "The biggest ever, so they say. My master's riding about inviting all the best knights to it."

"Really?" said Arthur.

"And that's not all," said the servant. "There's talk going around that at the end of the tournament the knights are going to choose a high king and put an end to the war. Of course, if you ask me ..."

Arthur didn't listen to the rest. He wasn't interested in the business about the High King but the thought of going to a great tournament made his heart beat faster. He'd never been to London – he'd be able to wear the new clothes he'd been given for his birthday, and – a sudden thought made him panic. He rushed into the castle, almost colliding with the messenger who was coming down the staircase, and burst into Sir Ector's private chamber.

Sir Ector and Sir Kay stared at him in astonishment.

"You can't!" panted Arthur. "I mean – you mustn't! It wouldn't be fair!"

"What are you babbling about, boy?" snapped Kay.

"The tournament in London," said Arthur. "You are going to take me, aren't you?"

Kay's eyes went small with anger. "How dare you talk that way!" he hissed. "How dare you burst into my father's chamber! I can see you need a good ducking in the horse trough!"

"Leave the boy alone, Kay," said Sir Ector firmly. "He's got himself so excited that he's forgotten his manners. I know someone else who used to do that at his age."

Kay closed his mouth tight.

Sir Ector turned to Arthur with a warm smile. "Yes, you're coming to the tournament," he said. "You're to be Kay's shield-bearer."

"Thank you, Father!" gasped Arthur.

"I've told you before about calling me Father, boy," Sir Ector said. "You must always call me Sir Ector."

"Yes, Sir Ector," Arthur mumbled.

"Now go down to the stables and tell the grooms to make the horses ready," said Sir Ector. "We're leaving for London at daybreak tomorrow."

he snow came in flurries and the cold wind rubbed Arthur's face raw, but he couldn't remember a time when he had been happier. In his young life he had never travelled so far before and it was like a dream.

Sir Ector, Kay and Arthur saw trim farmhouses. There were other knights and squires on the London road, and fine ladies riding inside silk-draped litters. They saw signs of war, too: burned-out villages whose ashes blackened the snow. Once, they had to move to the side of the road to let a band of lepers pass by.

They spent the first night in a monastery and Arthur fell asleep to the chanting of monks. The second night they stayed at an inn and Arthur hardly slept at all. He was kept awake by drunken voices singing songs with rude words.

On the morning of the third day they came to the outskirts of London and Arthur stopped his horse to gaze at the great city. In the distance he could see the tournament field which looked white because of all the tents pitched on it. Arthur felt excitement building up in his stomach and he urged his horse on.

A long way ahead, Sir Ector was talking to a knight he had met at the inn. Kay was dawdling behind, fiddling with his saddlebags and muttering under his breath. When Arthur drew level, Kay looked up, his face worried and pale.

"You haven't picked up my sword, have you?" he asked.

"No," said Arthur. "You told me that you'd set the hounds on me if I ever touched it, remember?"

Kay groaned and slapped himself on the forehead. "I've left it at the inn!" he groaned. "How could I be such an idiot? If I don't go back for it, I'll have no sword to use at the tournament and if I do go back, someone's bound to notice and ask me why. I'll be called Sir Kay the Forgetful for the rest of my days."

"Nobody would notice if I slipped away," said Arthur.

"You?" said Kay.

"I'll be back with the sword before anybody knows I've gone," Arthur vowed.

"All right," said Kay, "but, er, look, Arthur, you won't tell anyone else about this, will you?"

"I'm your brother," said Arthur. "I don't say bad things about you behind your back – well, not to other people, anyway."

Arthur felt happy as he galloped along the frosty road. Kay would be grateful to him when he brought the sword back. Perhaps he would be kind and behave more like a brother.

But when he reached the inn, Arthur's high hopes turned into dismay. The place was shut, the windows were boarded, the doors were barred and the only person in sight was an old man.

"Where's the innkeeper?" Arthur cried.

"Gone," replied the old man, "and taken 'is wife and 'is servants with 'im. They've all gone to the tournament, see. And where'm I goin' to get my mug of ale now, I'd like to know!"

"I didn't see them on the way," said Arthur. "What road have they taken?"

"That un," said the old man, pointing with his stick. "Past the cathedral churchyard, left at Gallows Field, right at the old kiln and then –"

Arthur didn't wait to hear any more. He turned his horse's head and kicked his heels into its sides.

It was hopeless. By the time he reached the churchyard, Arthur had forgotten what turning he was supposed to take next. If he carried on, he would only get lost.

He reined in his horse and came to a halt. There was no hope of Kay being kind now. Arthur had told his brother he would fetch his sword and he had let him down. The other young knights would make fun of Kay, and Kay would take it out on Arthur. And then, in the middle of all his dark thoughts, Arthur saw a sword.

t was the strangest of all the strange things Arthur had seen on the journey, but he hardly paid it any attention. In the centre of the churchyard stood a block of marble, white and glistening. There were golden letters carved in the marble, but Arthur didn't notice them. On top of the marble block was an iron anvil, but Arthur didn't really notice that either. All he could see was the sword. Its richly jewelled hilt glittered above the top of the anvil; its blade ran straight down through the iron into the marble beneath.

Arthur hadn't stopped before barging into Sir Ector's private chamber, and he didn't stop to think now. Kay needed a sword and there was a sword. The anvil and the marble block didn't matter a whistle.

Arthur scrambled out of his saddle, clambered over the churchyard wall and wove his way between the tombstones. When he reached the white marble block, he stretched out his right arm and closed his fingers on the sword's hilt. He could see no join between the steel of the blade and the iron of the anvil, and for a moment he thought he might not be able to lift it, but when he pulled, the sword ran out smoothly and rang like a chiming bell. Arthur bounded back to his horse, waving the sword over his head and whooping with delight.

Kay was waiting where Arthur had left him. When he saw the sword in Arthur's hand he grinned and Arthur thought the grin was worth all his worry and effort.

"Well done!" said Kay, taking the sword. "If we hurry, I can –"

He left the sentence unfinished. He was staring at the sword and there was an expression on his face that Arthur didn't recognise.

"This isn't my sword, Arthur!" Kay whispered. "Where did you get it?"

"The cathedral churchyard," said Arthur. "The inn was shut, so I asked this old man which way –"

"The messenger told us the sword had a jewelled hilt," said Kay, and though he spoke out loud he was really talking to himself, "and its blade had been driven deep into an anvil standing on a block of white marble ... "

"How did you know?" laughed Arthur.

Kay didn't answer. He rode off at full speed, shouting Sir Ector's name at the top of his voice. Arthur tried to follow, but his horse was tired and he soon lost sight of Kay in the crowds that were pressing towards the tournament field.

A short while later, Arthur met Kay and Sir Ector coming the other way. Kay looked nervous and Sir Ector's face was grim.

"Follow behind us, boy," muttered Sir Ector, "and don't say a word."

They rode together in silence and the silence didn't stop until they reached the cathedral churchyard. They tied their horses at the gate and Sir Ector led the way to the marble block and the anvil.

In front of the block, Sir Ector turned to Kay. "Is this where you got the sword?" he asked.

"Yes, Father." Kay spoke quietly and his lips were trembling.

"Kay," said Sir Ector, "when you became a knight it was the proudest day of my life. Don't make me ashamed of you now. Do you swear on your honour as a true knight that you drew the sword out of the anvil and the stone?"

Kay's eyes flicked from side to side. "No, Father," he admitted.

"Then where the devil did you get it?" bellowed Sir Ector.

"Arthur brought it to me."

"Arthur?" frowned Sir Ector. "What do you mean, Arthur brought it to you?"

"It's true, Father – I mean, Sir Ector!" said Arthur. "You see, Kay left his sword at the inn, so I said –"

"Never mind Kay's sword, boy! I want to know about this one!" shouted Sir Ector, shaking the sword with the jewelled hilt. "Where did you get it?"

"From the anvil," said Arthur. "I was passing the churchyard and I saw the sword. Kay needed it, so I got it for him. Did I do something wrong?"

Sir Ector offered the sword to Arthur. "Put it back," he said, and the quiet way he said it was somehow more frightening than a shout.

Arthur placed the point of the sword into the slit on top of the anvil and pushed it down as far as it would go.

"Try and take it out, Kay," said Sir Ector.

Kay pulled at the sword until the veins stood out on his temples, but he couldn't budge it.

Then Sir Ector tried. His face went red and his eyes bulged. At last he let go of the sword with a grunt of defeat.

"I might as well try to pull a stone out of the cathedral wall!" he said.

"But it's easy," said Arthur. "Look!"

This time the sword glided out as though the anvil had been carved out of black butter.

Sir Ector and Kay fell to their knees and bowed their heads.

"What's all this?" laughed Arthur. "Are you playing a joke on me?"

But when Sir Ector spoke, there was no joke in his voice. "You don't know what you've done, do you? Didn't you read the words in the marble?"

Arthur turned and looked. Now he saw how strange it all was: the churchyard, the bright steel of the sword, the dark iron of the anvil, the glistening marble and the golden letters that glowed:

'Whoever draws this sword from the anvil and the stone is the true-born High King of Britain.'

A SEA-SERPENT SAW A BIG TANKER

from Down in the Marvellous Deep
Sophie Windham

A sea-serpent saw a big tanker,
Bit a hole in her side and then sank her.
It swallowed the crew
In a minute or two,
And then picked its teeth with the anchor.

Anon

IVAN
AND THE
SEA KING

from The Orchard Book of Stories
from the Seven Seas

Pomme Clayton 🌀 Sheila Moxley

Once upon a time, on the shores of the Black Sea, there lived a
wealthy merchant and his three sons. The merchant owned a fleet of
ships and traded goods throughout Russia. His two eldest sons worked
with him, unloading and selling the cargo. But his youngest son, Ivan,
spent all day at the inn drinking vodka. And if he wasn't drinking
vodka, he was sleeping!

The older boys thought this was very unfair.

"Why should we do all the work," they complained, "while Ivan
does nothing?"

One day, down at the harbour, the merchant gave the two older
boys a fine ship each. The eldest son's ship was loaded with a cargo of
crisp linen. And the second son's ship was loaded with a cargo of
delicate tea.

"Thank you for your help, my boys," said the merchant. "Go and
make your fortunes."

But Ivan got nothing. He watched his brothers sail away, until their
ships were just specks on the horizon. Then he turned to his father
and begged, "Can I have a ship and a cargo?"

The merchant laughed. "Ivan, if I give you a cargo, you'll drink it all away."

"Oh please, Father, just a small ship. Then I can make my fortune too."

So the merchant gave Ivan a ship. A very small ship. With rotting timbers and ragged sails and a crew of ancient sailors – crusty old sea dogs. And as for cargo, there was none. Ivan bid his father goodbye and set sail towards his fortune.

The small ship coasted with the wind, while Ivan drank grog with the old sea dogs. But when the drink ran out, the sailors began to get grumpy. Ivan thought he'd better fill their stomachs to quieten their tempers. So he cast his fishing net overboard. When the net felt heavy he hauled it in and slung it on to the deck. There, struggling inside the net, was a golden octopus!

"I can sell you for a handsome price!" chuckled Ivan.

But the octopus cried out, "Please don't kill me. I am a prince, the son of the great Sea King, Chudo Yudo. Let me go and my father will bless you."

Ivan looked longingly at the golden octopus. He would never catch another one like it, and what use was a blessing anyway? He was just about to kill the octopus, when he remembered his own father. How sad he would be if he never saw his father again. Ivan picked up the octopus and flung it overboard.

Suddenly there was a rumbling sound and the sea began to swell. It was as if the bottom of the ocean was coming to the top. Out of the depths rose a glittering throne, and sitting on the throne was the great Sea King, Chudo Yudo. And he was huge! Half man and half octopus, with curling tentacles and a long grey beard, rich red gown and a golden crown on his head.

"As you helped my son," boomed the Sea King, "I will help you!"

He reached under his throne and pulled out a golden dish. "Fill this dish with sea water and leave it on the deck in the midday sun."

Then there was a rumbling and a bubbling, and the Sea King sank down under the waves.

Ivan filled the dish with sea water and placed it on the deck. The hot midday sun beat down and the water dried up. All that was left was a thin film of fine white powder lining the bottom of the dish. Ivan dipped his finger into the powder and licked it.

"Salt!" he cried. "The Sea King has shown me how to make salt!"

At once Ivan and the old sea dogs filled pans and pails with sea water and put them on the deck to dry. They worked hard filling pails and scraping out the crystals of salt. Until, after many days, the ship was overflowing with a cargo of the finest salt.

"We won't have any trouble selling this," cried Ivan. "Everyone wants salt!"

Now Ivan sailed! He sailed with the wind and he sailed against the wind, to the city of the Tsar, King of Russia. When they arrived at port, Ivan put a handful of salt into a little bag.

"My crew," he instructed, "guard the ship well. I'm going to the Tsar to ask for permission to trade."

And he put the bag of salt into his pocket.

Ivan was shown into the royal throne room. There was the Tsar and the Tsarina, and sitting between them on a golden footstool was their daughter the Tsarevna. Ivan bowed to the Tsar, and he secretly thought that the Tsarevna was the loveliest maiden he'd ever seen.

"Your Majesty," he said, "I am a merchant and I ask permission to trade in your city."

"What are you trading?" enquired the Tsar.

"Salt," said Ivan.

"Salt?" puzzled the Tsar. "What is that?"

Ivan pulled the bag out of his pocket and poured a little salt into the palm of his hand.

"You sprinkle it on your food," he said. "It tastes delicious!" And he offered the Tsar some salt. The Tsar dipped in his finger and licked it.

"UGGGH!" he spluttered. "It tastes disgusting! No one will buy that in my kingdom."

And Ivan was marched out of the palace.

Ivan was very downcast. "Someone must eat salt round here," he thought. "I'm going to find out!"

He went straight to the palace kitchen and begged for a glass of water. The chief cook took him inside and sat him by a roaring fire. Ivan sipped his water, then closed his eyes and pretended to go to sleep. But he peeped out from under his half-closed eyelashes and watched. The cooks were roasting, baking, stewing, frying, stirring and pouring. But no one was concerned with salting. Ivan waited until all the cooks were out of the kitchen. Then he went up to each pot and pan, and put a pinch of salt into every dish.

When the meal was served, the first course was the Tsar's favourite beetroot soup, and it tasted good. The Tsar smacked his lips, the Tsarina dabbed hers, and the Tsarevna licked hers, and they all had seconds! Then came the meat, it tasted excellent and they all had thirds! Then came a mountain of cakes that tasted divine. When the meal was finally over, the Tsar called for the chief cook.

"I've never tasted such a delicious meal in all my born days,"

relished the Tsar, patting his stomach. "What did you do?"

"Your Majesty," replied the cook, "we cooked it in exactly the same way as we always do."

"Nothing different?" asked the Tsar.

"Nothing – except for a merchant who sat by the fire sipping a glass of water."

"Bring me the merchant," ordered the Tsar.

Ivan bowed before the Tsar a second time.

"Oh! It's you," frowned the Tsar. "Did you put anything in the food?"

"Just a sprinkling of salt," said Ivan.

"You mean that terrible-tasting powder?"

"Yes, Your Majesty."

"Well I never!" cried the Tsar. "It made the soup soupier, the meat meatier, the vegetables vegetablier and the cake cakier. I will buy all the salt you have. How much do you want for it?"

"A bag of gold for each bag of salt," said Ivan quickly.

"Done!" cried the Tsar.

The sailors spent all day stuffing salt into bags. And all the next day carrying salt up to the palace. And all the day after that carrying gold down to the ship.

The maiden Tsarevna sat by her window and watched everything. She thought that Ivan was the cleverest man she'd ever met. And when Ivan bowed before the Tsar for the last time, she said sweetly, "Father, please can I go and look at Ivan's ship?"

The Tsar agreed, so Ivan took the Tsarevna by the hand and led her down to the harbour.

"It is only a small ship," he said, helping her aboard.

But the Tsarevna danced across the deck, admiring everything.

"What are those?" she asked, pointing at the rags hanging from the mast.

"The sails!" replied Ivan proudly. "Hoist the sails for the Tsarevna!" he called, and the old sea dogs hoisted the sails.

"But why aren't we moving?" she cried.

"Because of the anchor," answered Ivan.

"What's an anchor?"

"Weigh the anchor for the Tsarevna," shouted Ivan, and the old sea dogs hauled up the anchor. As the Tsarevna examined the anchor, the sails filled with wind and the ship lurched out of the harbour. The Tsarevna turned to Ivan and laughed. And the further out to sea they sailed, the happier she became!

"Oh, Ivan!" she sighed. "I could not bear to be without you."

Ivan and the Tsarevna sat down on a pile of gold and talked. Their talking turned to laughing, their laughing to kissing and in their kissing they fell in love. They were just planning their wedding, when Ivan saw two fine ships on the horizon. It was his brothers! Ivan steered his ship alongside theirs and invited them both aboard.

When the two brothers saw Ivan's gold, they could hardly believe their eyes. And when they met the Tsarevna, their eyes nearly popped out of their heads.

"It just isn't fair," they grumbled to each other. "We do all the work and Ivan gets the reward."

The two brothers were overcome with jealousy, and they hatched a terrible plan.

That night, when Ivan was keeping watch on deck, his brothers leapt upon him, bound a heavy weight to his feet and hurled him overboard.

"Now!" cried the eldest brother. "I will have the Tsarevna and you can have the gold!" And the two brothers shook hands greedily and sailed home as fast as they could.

Ivan sank like a stone, dragged down by the heavy weight. He sank deeper and deeper under the sea, and he began to drown. Suddenly, a long tentacle wrapped itself around Ivan's waist, gripped him tight and lifted him up through the water.

"As you helped my son, I will help you," boomed a voice.

It was Chudo Yudo, King of the Sea! He swept Ivan out of the water and placed him safely on a rack. Ivan coughed and spluttered and gasped for air, then he told the Sea King the whole story.

"Well," rumbled the Sea King, "we might just get to the church in time!"

And he lifted Ivan high up on his shoulders. Then he set off with giant strides, splashing and rushing through the foam. Ivan rode across the ocean on the shoulders of the Sea King. But by the time they reached the harbour, the church bells were already ringing. Ivan's eldest brother was about to marry the Tsarevna. Chudo Yudo placed Ivan on the shore.

"Ivan, promise me one thing," he said. "Never boast about riding on

my shoulders. If you do, I will hear you and destroy you."

Ivan bowed and promised not to tell a soul.

Then he ran to the church. The wedding march was playing, and
the Tsarevna was walking down the aisle looking very sad indeed.
But when she saw Ivan, she threw back her veil and cried, "That's
the true bridegroom over there!"

Everyone turned and looked at Ivan. And Ivan's father leapt to
his feet.

"Your brothers told me that you'd fallen overboard and drowned,"
he said, wiping away his tears. "Oh, how happy I am to see you
again!"

"I did not fall, Father," said Ivan. And he told all about the salt,
the gold, the Tsar's daughter and his brothers throwing him overboard.
At once the congregation began to shout.

"Kill those evil brothers!"

"Put them in a bottomless boat!"

"Push them out to sea!"

But Ivan took both his brothers by the hand and said softly, "No.
I understand exactly why you wanted me to drown, and I forgive
you. If you should die now, then this whole adventure would have
been for nothing."

Then Ivan turned to the congregation and said, "Let the real
wedding begin!"

So Ivan married the Tsarevna. And there was a huge wedding party,
with eating, dancing, singing, and storytelling. But most of all,
drinking vodka! Ivan went back to his old ways. He drank, the sea
dogs drank, and they all told jokes and boasted. They boasted about
how their ship was the finest, their horse was the fastest and their
daughter the cleverest. Then Ivan shouted at the top of his voice, "But
I'm the only one in the whole wide world who has ridden on the
shoulders of the Sea King!"

Hardly had the words slipped out of his mouth, when there was a
rumbling and a bubbling and the ground began to shake. A huge wave
crashed on the shore and Chudo Yudo, the King of the Sea, burst into
the hall.

"I heard you boasting, Ivan," he roared, "and I told you what would

happen if you did."

"Your Majesty," trembled Ivan. "Forgive me. It wasn't me boasting, it was the vodka!"

"What?" blazed the Sea King. "How can vodka boast?"

"I will show you," cried Ivan.

The old sea dogs rolled a barrel of vodka across the floor and tapped a hole in the top.

"Try it," said Ivan.

Chudo Yudo picked up the barrel, as if it were a drinking glass, and took a gulp.

"Mmmm, nice!" he grunted, and glugged down the whole barrel!

"Ecshellent... dilishussss..." he giggled.

The Sea King roared with laughter and staggered round the hall. He was drunk! He tumbled to the ground and rolled from side to side. He lashed his tentacles wildly and crushed all the feasting tables. The wedding guests scattered and Chudo Yudo flattened the whole hall. He uprooted trees, destroyed fields and smashed houses. Until, at last, he fell asleep. The Sea King slept for three days, and when he finally awoke he had a terrible headache!

"What has happened?" he moaned, staring at the devastation. "There must have been a terrible storm."

"A storm didn't do this," laughed Ivan. "You did!"

"It wasn't me who made the mess," bellowed the Sea King. "It was the vodka! And if vodka can do that much damage, then a little bit of boasting doesn't matter at all. You can boast about me for the next thousand years if you like!"

And Chudo Yudo stumbled into the sea and sank down under the waves.

Ivan looked at the damage and thought, "My brothers were right to want to drown me. I was drowning myself in all that vodka."

And he vowed never to touch another drop of vodka for the rest of his life. His brothers were very pleased about this. And they were even happier when Ivan repaired all the damage and built them each a new house.

Ivan and the Tsarevna lived a long and happy life. But Ivan did not give up boasting, the Sea King's boast lives on. For he told this tale to somebody, who told it to somebody, who told it to somebody, who told it to me. And as I have told it to you, what do you have to do?

WHAT IS POETRY?

from The Orchard Book of Poems • Chosen by Adrian Mitchell

Illustrations by Janie Coath

Reader: But what **is** poetry?
Adrian:

Poetry is a beautiful mud-pie
Washed down with a glassful of stars.

Poetry is one of the best ways
Of singing in the whole wide world
Or whispering in the ear of your best friend.

Poetry tunnels you out of your dungeon.
Poetry captures the three-headed dragon.
And teaches it Ludo and Frisbee-throwing.

Poetry is a Mammoth in a shopping mall,
A beggar with no legs in Disneyland,
A chocolate bicycle,
A truthburger with French flies
And the Moon's own telephone.

Poetry is your mind dancing
To the drumbeat of your heart.

Adrian Mitchell

Silver

Slowly, silently, now the moon
Walks the night in her silver shoon;
This way, and that, she peers, and sees
Silver fruit upon silver trees;
One by one the casements catch
Her beams beneath the silvery thatch;
Couched in his kennel, like a log,
With paws of silver sleeps the dog;
From their shadowy cote the white breasts peep
Of doves in silver-feathered sleep;
A harvest mouse goes scampering by,
With silver claws, and silver eye;
And moveless fish in the water gleam,
By silver reeds in a silver stream.

Walter de la Mare

What Is Pink?

What is pink? a rose is pink
By the fountain's brink.
What is red? a poppy's red
In its barley bed.
What is blue? the sky is blue
Where the clouds float thro'
What is white? a swan is white
Sailing in the light.
What is yellow? pears are yellow,
Rich and ripe and mellow.
What is green? the grass is green,
With small flowers between.
What is violet? clouds are violet,
In the summer twilight.
What is orange? why, an orange,
Just an orange!

Christina Rossetti

Song in Space

When man first flew beyond the sky
He looked back into the world's blue eye.
Man said: What makes your eye so blue?
Earth said: The tears in the oceans do.
Why are the seas so full of tears?
Because I've wept so many thousand years.
Why do you weep as you dance through space?
Because I am the Mother of the Human Race.

Adrian Mitchell

THE SLEEPING BEAUTY

from The Orchard Book of Stories from the Ballet

 Geraldine McCaughrean 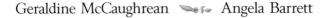 Angela Barrett

A baby daughter was once born to a king and queen. She was more beautiful than most, more happy than many, more loved than all but you. Her mother and father wanted her to have everything in life, and what was there to prevent it? They were rich, lived in a splendid palace, and numbered among their friends all the fairies of the forest and field. Fairies with rainbow wings and dresses of gossamer danced at the christening, when the baby was named Aurora, 'the dawn', because she seemed like a promise of a wonderful day to come.

Well, in fact, one fairy was missing, but then Carabosse had disappeared from the country in a huff of temper and a puff of smoke, and had not been seen for years.

358

So the fairies danced around the cradle like wisps of colour weaving themselves into a rainbow. And they laid their wands on the sleeping child and blessed her with Beauty, Wealth, Joy, Love and Grace.

"*And I have a present for her too!*" cried a voice.

It was the Fairy Carabosse, quite scarlet with fury, her wings trembling with rage. "Here, Princess," she sneered, tossing like a curse a glittering gift into the cradle. "One day, show what promise you may, win what hearts you might, let *that* be the death of you! Prick your finger and die!"

The other fairies snatched the golden spindle out of the crib, as though it were a poisonous snake. They hurled it out of the window. They begged Carabosse to take back her fearful curse. But the evil-tempered, proud fairy was so offended at having been forgotten, overlooked, that no amount of tears could move her to pity.

"Then I must undo your mischief!" cried the Lilac Fairy, flittering from behind a curtain. "You thought your wicked gift was the last, but I still have mine to give! And though I can't undo your cruel magic, I can blunt its spiteful point. Let the Princess not die when she pricks her finger; let her sleep for a hundred years. Then, while she sleeps, let her blessings grow, so that she wakes to yet more joy than her friends can wish her today!"

Carabosse fumed and seethed. She stormed out, slamming the great doors with a noise that shook the very stones of the palace and the very hearts of the guests. But she was no sooner gone than she was forgotten, for the world has no wish to remember the wicked, only the good and the lovely.

Even so, King Floristan banished all spindles and spinning wheels from his kingdom, to make sure Princess Aurora could never prick her finger on one.

In the space of sixteen years, Aurora grew into such a princess as fairy tales are made of. She was beautiful and kind, loved by everyone she met, the pride of her tutors and the joy of her friends. When she danced, the flowers reached higher out of the ground to peep in at the windows.

Princes travelled from all over the world, half in love with the thought of her, instantly in love at the sight of her. At her sixteenth birthday party, four princes presented their compliments to King Floristan and begged for the hand of Princess Aurora in marriage.

"You must ask her yourselves," said her parents. "We wouldn't choose to part with her for all the world, but it is time she spread happiness beyond the bounds of this small kingdom, and enjoyed the happiness of married life as well."

So the Prince of England and the Prince of Spain and the Prince of India and the Prince of France bowed low to the Princess Aurora and partnered her in dancing. Each one thought he had won her heart.

"She smiled such a smile at me!"

"She held my hand so tenderly!"

"She danced as though her heart was on fire!"

"She laughed at *all* my jokes!"

And yet it was just Aurora's nature to make her friends and guests feel welcome. She was overbrimming with love – but not for any one man more than another.

So it was that she greeted the strange old woman shrouded in grey and cradling something in her arms. "A birthday present for you, my dear," croaked the old crone.

"Do I know you? How very kind. Every one has been so kind to me today," said Aurora. "What is it?"

About the size of a newborn baby, and almost as light, it was

wrapped in cloth as black as spite. But as Aurora unwrapped it, the present glittered with the yellow of gold, the spangle of fleecy golden yarn, the silver sliver of a sharp needle. It was a spindle for spinning wool into yarn.

"Aurora, don't touch it!" cried her mother.

"Ow! Look, I've pricked my finger. You'd best take it from me. I shall put blood on the pretty wool."

Suddenly the room began to swim and melt, the floor to heave and the ceiling to bow.

"So tired," said Aurora, then fell flat, so deeply asleep that she did not even put out her hands to stop herself from falling.

"Carabosse, your spite has made you the shame of Fairyland. No tongue will ever speak to you again. No face will ever smile your

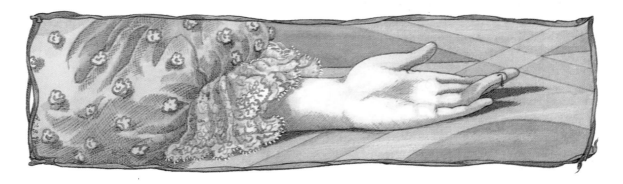

way. Leave here for ever." For a moment, Carabosse stood face to face with the Lilac Fairy, then, with a furious stamp of her foot, she was gone.

The King and Queen were sobbing; the Princes had all drawn their swords; Aurora's friends leaned over her, powerless to wake her. "Carry her to bed!" commanded the Lilac Fairy. "Have you forgotten her fate? To sleep for one hundred years?"

"Then she might as well be dead, for we shall never see her dance or smile again," sobbed the King. "We shall all be dead long since when she opens her eyes again."

But it was not the Lilac Fairy's intention to keep only Aurora safe, swaddled in dreamless sleep. She swept her wand over the heads of the courtiers and ladies-in-waiting, the princes and guests, the King and Queen. And one by one they fell asleep where they stood or sat or sprawled or knelt, sinking into sleep like the leaves settling to the ground from an autumn tree.

And as the Court of King Floristan sank down, up sprang a

hedge round his palace; trees and brambles and briars and bushes conjured out of the ground by the Lilac Fairy's wand. They buried the palace steps, they smothered the palace windows, they muffled its high turrets. The topmost branches stretched protective twigs over the tiled roofs, so that the entire building was smothered in creepers and thorns. So dense was the greenery that a stranger riding by might see no palace there at all.

Of course the people who lived in the villages near by knew of the palace, knew that their king and queen and princess were lost somewhere inside the magic barricade of trees. At first they talked of nothing else. The wonder of it filled their every thought. They tried to get in – failed every time – said the thorns were sharp as needles, the creepers unbreakable.

But there were pigs to feed, the corn to be cut, the sheep to shear, the roof to patch. And people forgot the most marvellous things after a few busy years. Those who had ever seen King Floristan, his courtiers and his lovely daughter grew old and died.

After sixty or seventy years the palace in the wood was only a rumour, a legend, a fairy story half believed, about a sleeping beauty and a magic spell.

Exactly one hundred years after Aurora's sixteenth birthday, a young prince called Charmant rode by on the highway with his friends. The forest seemed a pleasant place for a picnic. There was suddenly a flicker of movement among the trees.

"A deer!" cried the Prince's aide. "Let's hunt it!"

The others were eager enough, but somehow Prince Charmant had no taste for the hunt. When his friends all rushed away into the tangled undergrowth, he remained behind. "What is this place?" he wanted to know. "Why does it give me such a strange feeling? Why does it make my heart beat faster?"

"They say there is a palace in the heart of the forest," said a voice.

"Who are you? Where did you come from? I didn't see you before."

"And in the heart of the palace a room," said the girl in the lilac dress. "And at the heart of the room a bed."

"And at the heart of the bed?"

"A beautiful princess. Sleeping."

The Prince leapt up and rushed at the wall of dense green: knotted creepers, tangles of thorn, fallen branches, barricades of tree trunks and, underfoot, slippery moss. "Do you know these parts? Can you show me a way through? Is there a way through?" he begged to know.

"For you? Oh yes. I believe so," said the girl in lilac, and idly breaking off a wand of grass crowned with a star of thistledown, she began to pick her way through the tangled undergrowth. Charmant kept close, following in her footsteps. And strangely

enough, the thorns (though they were sharp as needles) never once snagged her lilac dress, nor scratched his own face or hands.

Suddenly his boots stumbled against steps, steps rising upwards to the mossy splendour of an arched doorway. No lock kept him out. No guard challenged him. All the candles had burned down to their holders. All the firegrates were snowy with ash.

In every doorway, passageway and chair, people lay fast asleep. But the girl in lilac did not seem to think them important, for she

led him onwards to a bedroom in the heart of the palace. There, in the heart of a snowy bed, untouched by cobwebs, lay a young girl. She was dressed in her finest clothes, as if for a party, and her beautiful face was tilted upwards as if awaiting a kiss.

Strange, to kiss a stranger, especially a stranger lying unconscious in an enchanted palace. And yet he could not help it. It seemed as if Charmant's whole life had been one long wait for this particular day, for this particular kiss.

As their lips touched, her eyes flew open, and his fate was sealed. Beautiful in her sleep, his Sleeping Beauty was still more lovely half awake.

She stirred. She sat up. She put her feet gingerly to the ground and looked around, puzzled at finding herself so far from the party. And yet she did not look around as much as she might, for she could hardly bear to look away from the face of Prince Charmant. Had he kissed her? What a saucy liberty to take, uninvited! And yet she thought her heart would burst if he did not kiss her again.

Throughout the palace, courtiers and ladies-in-waiting stretched

and yawned, rubbed stiff necks, puzzled at how they could possibly have fallen asleep at the height of the birthday party. Then they remembered. The King and Queen hugged one another as they remembered. It was a strange feeling to go to sleep and wake up one hundred years later.

"Am I old and hideous?" asked the Queen.

"Not a day older than ... than ... than when I last saw you," said the King. "Not one hour. Not one minute."

The orchestra began to pluck their instruments – and found them in tune, even after a century's silence.

The spell was broken. The trees melted away from round the

palace like clematis dying back for the winter months. The thorns melted like spiky frost. The dense leaves flew away like a flock of a million green birds, into a cloudless sky.

All the fairies in Fairyland were invited to the wedding, just as they had been invited to the christening. Even Carabosse was invited, to see how her evil had been turned to good. But though a herald searched the whole kingdom and far beyond, there was no trace of Carabosse – only a few bitter aloes growing where her gossamer hammock had once hung.

And what more natural at a wedding blessed by fairies, than that the characters of fairy tales should come along as guests: Tom Thumb, Puss in Boots, Red Riding Hood, Beauty and her Beast. After the ceremony and the dancing, these famous celebrities told their stories as the new candles glimmered in a thousand candelabras, and the wedding guests listened, entranced. Only Aurora and her Prince Charmant remained dancing, held in Love's spell for evermore.

THE UNICORN WHO
WALKS ALONE

from The Orchard Book of Mythical Birds and Beasts

Margaret Mayo Jane Ray

The Unicorn is a beautiful and mysterious beast who always walks alone. He is rarely seen. But once – and *only* once – the Unicorn did come among the other animals. And that one and only time he shared with them his strange and magical powers.

Far, far away there was a wood, and under the shady trees there was a pool of fresh water. It was the animals' pool, where they all came to drink.

Now for months there had been no rain and the sun had shone,
hot and fierce. The streams and rivers dried up. The grass turned
yellowy-brown. Even the weeds frizzled up and died. But the
animals' pool, under the shady trees, stayed full to the brim.
It never failed. And so the animals had enough water to drink.

Until, one day, a serpent came slithering out of a cave. He
moved fast across the dry grass, into the wood and straight
towards the animals' pool. When he reached the water's edge,
he slowly raised his head and swaying from side to side, stretched
over the pool and spurted out a flood of deadly poison. It floated
across the surface like oil, covering the whole of the pool. Then
the serpent moved off, fast as he came, back to his cave.

And why did the serpent do this? Because he was wicked.
Because he felt like it. And because he cared for
no one but himself. That was why.

At their usual times the animals sauntered along in ones or twos or friendly little groups towards the pool. But as soon as they reached the waters edge, they smelt the poison and saw it floating on the surface, and they knew that if they swallowed it, they would die.

Some animals were so upset they moaned quietly. Others yelped and roared their anger. Not one turned back and left.

By evening there was a huge crowd round the pool. Animals who were definitely *not* good friends and who *never* drank together were side by side: the lion, the buffalo and the antelope, the wolf, the camel, the donkey and the sheep ... and many more besides.

Night came, the moon rose in the sky, and still more animals came. From time to time some would call out and then others would add their voices to the loud, mournful cry. Each time the cry grew louder. Was there no one who could help them?

The Unicorn, the beautiful one who walks alone, was far off, but at last he heard the animals' cry. He listened and understood. He kicked up his hoofs and came trotting, slowly at first, but steadily gaining speed until he was galloping faster than the wind.

As he approached the wood he slowed down, and then stepping softly, he wound his way in and out among the trees. He saw the animals gathered round the pool. He smelt the poison. Then he knew everything.

The Unicorn knelt beside the pool, lowered his head and dipped his long pointed horn into the water, deeper and deeper, until it was completely covered. He waited a moment and then slowly lifted his horn out of the water. He stood up. His magical horn had done its work. The poison was gone. The water was fresh and pure again.

Without pushing, nudging or quarrelling of any kind, the animals lowered their heads and drank. When their thirst was quenched and their strength returned, they all called out with one voice, their thanks to the Unicorn.

But he was not there. He had left while they were drinking. His work was done. He needed no one. He was the Unicorn who walks alone.

A traditional European story

The Happy Prince

from the fairy tale by Oscar Wilde

Jane Ray

High above the city, on a tall column, stood the statue of the Happy Prince. He was gilded all over with thin leaves of fine gold, for eyes he had two bright sapphires, and a large red ruby glowed on his sword-hilt.

One night there flew over the city a little Swallow. He saw the statue on the tall column. So he alighted just between the feet of the Happy Prince.

"I have a golden bedroom," he said to himself, as he prepared to go to sleep; but just as he was putting his head under his wing, a large drop of water fell on him. Then another drop fell. A third drop fell, and he looked up.

The eyes of the Happy Prince were filled with tears, and tears were running down his golden cheeks. His face was so beautiful in the moonlight that the little Swallow was filled with pity.

"Who are you?" he said.

"I am the Happy Prince."

"Why are you weeping then?" asked the Swallow. "You have quite drenched me."

"When I was alive and had a human heart," answered the statue, "I did not know what tears were. My courtiers called me the Happy Prince. And now that I am dead, they have set me here so high that I can see all the misery of my city, and though my heart is made of lead I cannot choose but weep."

"Far away," continued the statue, "is a poor house. In a bed a little boy is lying ill. He is asking for oranges. His mother has nothing to give him but river water, so he is crying. Swallow, little Swallow, will you not bring her the ruby out of my sword-hilt?"

"I am waited for in Egypt," said the Swallow. "My friends are flying up and down the Nile, and talking to the lotus flowers. Soon they will go to sleep in the tomb of the great King. The King is there himself in his painted coffin. Round his neck is a ring of pale green jade, and his hands are like withered leaves."

"Swallow, Swallow, little Swallow," said the Prince, "will you not stay with me for one night, and be my messenger?"

The Happy Prince looked so sad that the little Swallow picked out the great ruby from the Prince's sword, and flew away with it in his beak over the roofs of the town.

He passed by the cathedral tower, where the white marble angels were sculptured. He passed over the river, and saw the lanterns hanging from the masts of the ships. At last he came to the poor house where the little boy lay ill and dropped the ruby on to the table.

Then he flew back to the Happy Prince, and told him what he had done. "It is curious, but I feel quite warm now, although it is so cold."

When the moon rose the next day the Swallow looked up at the Happy Prince. "I am starting for Egypt," he said.

"Swallow, Swallow, little Swallow," said the Prince, "will you not stay with me just one night longer?"

"I am waited for in Egypt," answered the Swallow. "There, on a great granite throne sits the God Memnon. All night long he watches the stars, and when the morning star shines he utters one cry of joy, and then is silent. At noon the yellow lions come down to the water's edge to drink."

"Swallow, Swallow, little Swallow," said the Prince, "far away across the city I see a young man in a garret. He is trying to finish a play for the Director of the Theatre, but he is too cold to write any more."

"I will wait with you one night longer," said the Swallow, who really had a good heart. "Shall I take him another ruby?"

"Alas! I have no ruby now," said the Prince. "My eyes are all that I have left. They are made of rare sapphires fron India. Pluck one of them out and take it to him."

"Dear Prince," said the Swallow, "I cannot do that," and he began to weep.

"Swallow, Swallow, little Swallow," said the Prince, "do as I command you."

So the Swallow plucked out the Prince's eye, and flew away to the student's garret. And when the student looked up he saw the sapphire lying on his desk.

"I must bid you goodbye," cried the Swallow, when the moon rose the next night. "I am going to Egypt!"

"Swallow, Swallow, little Swallow," said the Prince, "will you not stay with me just one night longer?"

"It is winter," answered the Swallow, "and the snow will soon be here. In Egypt the sun is warm on the palm trees and the crocodiles lie in the mud and look lazily about them. Dear Prince, I must leave you, but next spring I will bring you back two beautiful jewels in place of those you have given away."

"In the square below," said the Happy Prince, "there stands a little match girl. She has let her matches fall in the gutter. She has no shoes or stockings, and her little head is bare. Pluck out my other eye, and give it to her."

"I will stay with you one night longer," said the Swallow, "but I cannot pluck out your eye. You would be quite blind then."

"Swallow, Swallow, little Swallow," said the Prince, "do as I command you."

So the Swallow plucked out the Prince's other eye, darted down with it and slipped the jewel right into the palm of the little match girl's hand.

Then the Swallow came back to the Prince. "You are quite blind now," he said, "so I will stay with you always."

All the next day he sat on the Prince's shoulder, and told him stories of what he had seen in strange lands. He told him of the red ibises, who stand in long rows on the banks of the Nile, and catch goldfish in their beaks; of the Sphinx, who is as old as the world itself and lives in the desert, and knows everything; of the great green snake that sleeps in a palm tree; and of the King of the Mountains of the Moon, who is as black as ebony, and worships a large crystal.

"Dear little Swallow," said the Prince, "you tell me of marvellous things but there is no mystery so great as misery. Fly over my city, little Swallow, and tell me what you see there."

So the Swallow flew over the great city and saw the rich merry-making in their beautiful houses while the beggars were sitting at their gates. Then he flew back and told the Prince what he had seen.

"I am covered with fine gold," said the Prince. "You must take it off leaf by leaf, and give it to the poor."

Leaf after leaf of the fine gold the Swallow picked off, till the Happy Prince looked quite dull and grey. Leaf after leaf of the fine gold he brought to the poor, and the children's faces grew rosier, and they laughed and played games in the street.

Then the snow came, and after the snow came the frost. Everybody went about in furs, and the little boys wore scarlet caps and skated on the ice.

The poor little Swallow grew colder and colder, but he would not leave the Prince. He loved him too well.

But at last he knew he was going to die. "Goodbye, dear Prince!" he murmured. And he kissed the Happy Prince and fell down dead at his feet.

At that moment a curious crack sounded inside the statue. The leaden heart had snapped right in two. It certainly was a dreadfully hard frost.

Early next morning the Mayor was walking in the square below with his town councillors. "Dear me! How shabby the Happy Prince looks!" he said. "And there is actually a dead bird at his feet!" he continued. "We must issue a proclamation that birds are not allowed to die here."

So they pulled down the statue of the Happy Prince. Then they melted the statue in a furnace. But the broken heart would not melt, so it was thrown on a dust heap where the little Swallow was also lying.

"Bring me the two most precious things in the city," said God to one of his angels; and the angel brought him the leaden heart and the dead bird.

"You have rightly chosen," said God, "for in my garden of Paradise this little bird shall sing and the Happy Prince shall live for evermore."

The Girl who did Some Baking

from The Orchard Book of Creation Stories

Margaret Mayo ❤ Louise Brierley

Have you ever wondered why children come in all sorts of different colours? Well, have you? It's because of something that happened long ago. In that far-off time, there was no earth and it was always dark. But high above the black night sky, in a place that was full of night, lived Nyame, the Sky God. And inside Nyame there lived some spirit people.

Now Nyame liked making things, and a time came when he decided to make something very special. First he took an enormous basket and filled it with earth and planted it with every kind of

385

wonderful plant. But that was not enough for Nyame. He then made lots of splendid animals and birds and insects, and set them among the plants.

When he had finished, Nyame stood back and admired his earth basket. "That's certainly something special!" he said. "And I know exactly where I'm going to put it!"

He carefully cut a round hole in the sky, and then he made a trap door that fitted the hole. He opened the trap door. He tied a rainbow rope to the basket and lowered it through the hole, down and down, until it reached the place where the earth basket is today.

Light flooded through the hole and lit up everything down below – and that hole is the round sun, which still lights up the earth when Nyame's trap door is open.

Nyame was pleased with his work, and he looked down and admired it some more. But after a while he closed the trap door, and immediately it was black night down on the earth basket. "Oh, my poor animals!" said Nyame. "I had forgotten about them! They will be so frightened in the dark!"

There and then, he cut some extra holes in the sky – and those holes are the moon and stars, which still shine when Nyame's trap door is shut.

Nyame was fond of this earth basket, and he was constantly opening the trap door and looking down. Sometimes one or two of the spirit people who lived inside him would climb up into his mouth, and then they would look down as well.

One day, when Nyame was admiring his earth basket, he noticed a bare patch where nothing was growing. "I must fill that up!" he said.

So he took a small basket, the same size as the empty space, and

he filled it with plants. He tied a rainbow rope to the basket, and then began to lower it through the hole in the sky.

Now one of the girl spirits who lived inside Nyame was called Iyaloda. She was lively and interested in just about everything. As soon as she heard that Nyame was lowering a small basket, she said to the boy spirit who was her special friend, "Let's go and have a look!"

"Hmmm … all right," he said. And hand in hand, they crept up inside Nyame.

When they came to his mouth, Iyaloda and the boy spirit tiptoed over his tongue, up to his teeth and leaned out over his big lips. And the next moment Nyame *sneezed!* and Iyaloda and the boy spirit where whirled out of his mouth, down through the hole and plump into the middle of the small basket.

By the time they had got their breath back, the small basket had landed and somehow fitted itself into the empty space in the earth basket.

"That was a bit unexpected," said Iyaloda. "But now we

are here let's look around."

The two of them set off, hand in hand. At first they were quite happy. There were so many wonderful things to see. But it was not long before they began to wonder how they could get back to their home inside Nyame. They thought and thought, but they could not think of a way to reach the trap door up in the sky. And then they felt sad.

When darkness came, and the moon and stars began to shine, they made a shelter with some branches, curled up close to one another and fell asleep.

As the days went by, Iyaloda and the boy spirit often felt real, deep-down sad. It was lonely living by themselves, far away from Nyame and all their spirit friends. Sometimes the boy spirit would wander off and comfort himself by talking to the wind and the trees, and then dancing a lonesome dance. But when Iyaloda, the girl spirit, felt sad, she sat and she thought, and she thought. At last, one day, she had a really clever thought.

When the boy spirit came back, Iyaloda was excited. She said,

all in a rush, "I have had a really clever thought."

"Iyaloda," sighed the boy spirit, "I don't want to hear it. Your clever thoughts always lead to trouble. Remember the last one... *'Let's creep up into Nyame's mouth'*. That's how we got sneezed down here!"

"This is a sensible thought," said Iyaloda. "Listen, we could make some little ones. Like us. We could call them children. Then we wouldn't be lonely any more."

"And how could we do that?" asked the boy spirit.

"We could dig out some clay and make little models that looked like us and bake them in a fire. Then we could breathe life into them."

"I suppose," said the boy spirit slowly, "I suppose it wouldn't do any harm to try..."

"Let's start making them now," said Iyaloda.

So they dug out clay and made models of little boy children and little girl children, rather like themselves. Then they built a big pile of wood round the models and set it alight.

But Iyaloda was impatient, and it wasn't long before she said, "They must be ready now. Let's look!" And she covered the fire with big green leaves to dampen it down.

When everything was cool, she took out the clay models. Some were pale white, some were pinkish white and some were creamy white. Each one a little different.

"Oh, they *are* beautiful!" said Iyaloda. "Let's make some more!" So the next day they dug more clay, made more models, and built a fire and set it alight.

"This time," said Iyaloda, "I shall bake them for a good while longer and see what happens."

She waited and she waited, and that was something that Iyaloda found hard to do. But at last she decided that the models had had a long enough bake, and she covered the fire with leaves.

When everything was cool, she took out the models. This time some were deep black, some were rich dark brown and some were reddish brown. Each one a little different.

"Oh they *are* beautiful!" said Iyaloda. "Let's make some more!" So the next day they made more models, and set the fire alight again.

"This time," said Iyaloda, "I won't give them a short bake or a long bake. They shall have an in-between bake!"

She waited, and as soon as she thought the models had been baked for an in-between time, she covered the fire with leaves.

And when she took out these models, some were golden yellow, and some were golden brown. Each one a little different.

"Oh they *are* beautiful!" said Iyaloda. "Let's make ..."

"No!" said the boy spirit. "We have enough children already! The time has come to breathe life into them."

Then they knelt down and breathed life into each one in

turn, and each little clay model came to life, like children waking from a long sleep. So the boy spirit and Iyaloda, the girl spirit, became the first father and the first mother and, because they had their big family to look after and love, they never again felt lonely.

And, of course, from those first children came all the children of the world, in all their different and beautiful colours.

A West African Story

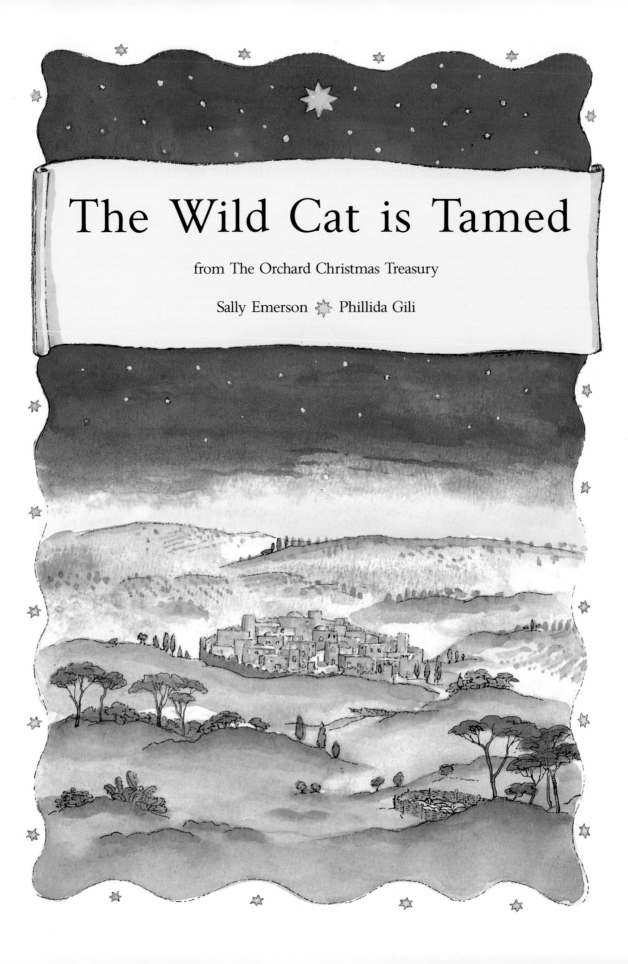

The Wild Cat is Tamed

from The Orchard Christmas Treasury

Sally Emerson ✳ Phillida Gili

It is said that the ox in the stable at Bethlehem did not eat the fresh hay in her manger so that Mary could use it for the baby's bed, and a sheep gave Mary wool so that she could weave a soft blanket. Even a small brown beetle joined in the worship of the new baby. Only Jesus noticed the beetle because it was so tiny, touching it with his finger. Ever since then the glow-worm, it is said, has shone with a bright light to guide travellers through the night.

The cat, too, has a story told about what happened to her on the night Jesus was born.

The cat used to be wild. She stayed out in the forest at night, hiding in trees, watching with her bright eyes. She was often afraid. She was especially wary of humans.

But one night she heard the news that a special human had been born in a stable near by. She wanted to go and see the baby but she was afraid to. For a long time she slunk around the forest, trying as usual to be invisible.

A squirrel came running by. "The son of God has just been born, the son of God has just been born," cried out the squirrel to the leaves and the insects and the birds. The whole forest was full of a rustle and a whirl.

"Oh, I would so like to go," purred the cat to herself.

"Underneath the star," cried out an eagle. "He's been born in a stable underneath the giant star."

The cat crept through the bushes and trees, looking this way and

that, until she came to the stable under the star. She slid under the door to join the other animals adoring the baby who lay in a manger.

The baby wasn't like the other humans the cat had seen. This one was different and made the cat feel peaceful.

The cat moved like a shadow behind the other animals of the forest, who were all worshipping the baby. She hoped no one would see her; she just wanted to be silent and to watch.

But one by one the other animals left to look for food or to sleep. The cat was uneasy to be left with the baby and the mother, but still she stayed. Although the cat liked solitude, she felt the mother and baby might need her companionship.

"Little cat," called Mary, after the deer, the fox, the pheasant, the squirrel and the rabbit had gone. "Little cat," she called again.

The cat came out from its hiding-place behind a bale of straw.

"Sweet cat. Don't try to be invisible." Mary laughed. Her laughter was – oh – like sunlight on fur, warm and comforting.

"Little cat – only you among all the wild animals of the forest has stayed to keep me company."

The cat approached, slowly, stealthily. Mary's smile made her feel happy, and she rubbed up against Mary's blue gown to be stroked and didn't feel quite so lonely.

"Thank you for staying with us. From now on you will be part of the lives of humans, and not have to prowl through the night for your food."

The cat purred, and thought that sounded good. She curled up and fell into the sweetest sleep she had ever known.

Cats – as their reward from Mary, it is said – no longer have to prowl hungrily through the shadows of the forest, their claws ready to attack. Instead they curl up in the front of cosy fires made by humans who love them and feed them.

But sometimes they still like to stalk the night streets, chasing shadows, jumping at every sound, their eyes bright and strange, remembering how things used to be.

ACKNOWLEDGEMENTS

The editor and publishers would like to thank the following for the use of copyright material in this collection. All books cited are originally published by Orchard Books.

HUMPTY DUMPTY AND OTHER RHYMES from THE ORCHARD BOOK OF NURSERY RHYMES © illustrations Faith Jaques, 1986; MY CLOTHES from MY FIRST ENGLISH FRENCH WORD BOOK © text and illustrations Venice Shone, 1993; GETTING DRESSED from BABY DAYS © illustrations Carol Thompson, 1991; THIS LITTLE BABY'S POTTY from the book of the same name © text and illustrations Lynn Breeze, 1992; ONE HUNGRY BABY from the book of the same name © text Lucy Coats, 1992 © illustrations Susan Hellard, 1992; PINK SOCK, PURPLE SOCK from the book of the same name © text and illustrations Jonathan Allen, 1992. Reprinted in the USA by permission of William Morrow & Company, Inc.; FIVE LITTLE DUCKS from the book of the same name © illustrations Ian Beck, 1992. In the USA, from FIVE LITTLE DUCKS by Ian Beck, © 1992, Ian Beck. Reprinted by permission of Henry Holt & Co., Inc.; THIS LITTLE BABY GOES SHOPPING from the book of the same name © text and illustrations Lynn Breeze, 1991; HEADS AND SHOULDERS from BABY DAYS © illustrations Carol Thompson, 1991; 123 HOW MANY ANIMALS CAN YOU SEE? from the book of the same name © text and illustrations Emilie Boon, 1987. In the USA, 123 HOW MANY ANIMALS CAN YOU SEE? by Emilie Boon. Copyright © 1987 by Emilie Boon. Reprinted by permission of Orchard Books, New York; HELPING from the book of the same name © text and illustrations Catherine Anholt, 1991; FOUR FIERCE KITTENS from the book of the same name © text Joyce Dunbar, 1991 © illustrations Jakki Wood, 1991. Reprinted in the USA by permission of Scholastic Inc.; THE WEATHER AND ME BY FRED CAT from the book of the same name © text and illustrations Jonathan Allen, 1997; THE ORCHARD ABC from the book of the same name © text and

illustrations Ian Beck, 1994. GOING TO PLAYGROUP from the book of the same name © text Laurence Anholt, 1991 © illustrations Catherine Anholt, 1991; BIG OWL, LITTLE TOWEL from the book of the same name © text and illustrations Jonathan Allen, 1992. Reprinted in the USA by permission of William Morrow & Company, Inc.; MR BEAR'S PLANE from the book of the same name © text and illustrations Colin & Jacqui Hawkins, 1989; LITTLE PIGLET from the book of the same name © text and illustrations Nicola Smee, 1996; THE THREE LITTLE PIGS from the ORCHARD BOOK OF NURSERY STORIES © text and illustrations Sophie Windham, 1991; WELLIE BEAR from TEDDY TALES © text Sally Grindley, 1993 © illustrations Peter Utton, 1993; BATHTIME from FIRST RHYMES © text Lucy Coats, 1994 © illustration Selina Young, 1994; THE BIG SHIP SAILS illustration from FIRST RHYMES © illustration Selina Young, 1994; PLASTIC PENGUIN'S STORY from TOYBOX TALES © text Sally Grindley, 1996 © illustrations Andy Ellis, 1996; LITTLE CHICK from the book of the same name © text and illustrations Nicola Smee, 1986; THE CHRISTMAS STORY from the book of the same name © text and illustrations Nicola Smee, 1994. Reprinted in the USA by permission of William Morrow & Company, Inc.; TWINKLE, TWINKLE, LITTLE STAR and STAR LIGHT STAR BRIGHT illustrations from FIRST RHYMES and FIRST POEMS © illustrations Selina Young, 1994; BILLY AND THE BRILLIANT BABYSITTER from the book of the same name © text Hiawyn Oram, 1994 © illustrations Sonia Holleyman, 1994; LITTLE MOUSE TWITCHY WHISKERS from the book of the same name © text Margaret Mayo, 1992 © illustrations Penny Dann, 1992; SOMETHING SPECIAL from the book of the same name © text Nicola Moon, 1995 © illustrations Alex Ayliffe, 1995. Reprinted in the USA by permission of Peachtree Publishers Ltd.; POEMS FROM RUMBLE IN THE JUNGLE from RUMBLE IN THE JUNGLE © text Giles Andreae, 1996 © illustrations David Wojtowycz, 1996. Reprinted in Ireland (Republic of Ireland &